the hypnotherapy

All rights reserved. No part of this publication may be reproduced in any form (including electronically) without the written permission of the copyright owner except in accordance with the provisions of the Copyright Designs and Patents Act 1988.
Application for permission to reproduce should be directed to the publisher.
ISBN-13: 978-1518601682
ISBN-10: 1518601685

Published by Ann Jaloba Publishing, 26 Tapton Mount Close, Sheffield S10 5DJ

copyright © Ann Jaloba Publishing
the moral right of the author has been asserted
Cover image I -stockliravega

DEDICATION

I would like to dedicate this book to everyone who has benefited from the skills and knowledge of the therapists who write here (including myself).

Without you our efforts would be worthless.

About the editor

Ann has a spent her whole career writing, editing and authoring health and wellbeing journals, books, websites and magazines. She is a qualified hypnotherapist and supervisor and coaches and supports entrepreneurs who want to write for publication.

Ann has worked on award winning journals for the Royal College of Nursing, including the best-selling weekly *Nursing Standard*. She is the former editor of the *The Hypnotherapy Journal*.

Her books include *FirstDays: how to set up a therapy business and stay sane*, designed to help new therapists through that tricky first year in business. She co-edited *The Hypnotherapy Handbook*, a comprehensive guide to the major client issues in hypnotherapy which features chapters by many of the UK's leading hypnotherapists. Her latest collaboration is *The Pocket Book of Stress Busters*, a simple and powerful set of techniques to help anyone cope.

She is an accredited (NCFE recognised) supervisor and supervises and coaches many therapists from beginners to Harley Street experts. She runs SupervisionPlus, a service offering supervision, peer support, information and training and PractisePlus, an online training organisation offering continuing professional development at all levels.

You can contact Ann at www.yourbookforbusiness.com

the hypnotherapy experts

CONTENTS

Meet the Hypnotherapy Experts

Foreword by Peter Mabbut

Introduction by Ann Jaloba

Part One: Specialise: the best route to success

Business brilliance: why you should choose a niche   3

Choosing your niche and selling products   19

Part Two: Choosing the best niche for you

Hypnosis and fertility go naturally together   39

Axeing addictions: breaking the addictive cycle   57

Changing the mindset of the anxious executive	71
Developing a specialist niche in coaching	87
From fear of flying to flying fabulously	90
Tinnitus, dealing with a complicated condition	111
Manage, control and abolish anxiety	128

Part Three: Nicheing in weightloss

Man up lose weight: a male perspective is different	145
"I build confidence and clients lose weight"	161
Helping the Asian community slim down	177
GET YOUR COMPLIMENTARY EXTRAS	194

Meet The Hypnotherapy Experts

All our contributors have made a success by specialising in a particular field and becoming an expert. They tell you what they do, how they do it and why it works

Steve Miller is a very well known clinical hypnotherapist, author, TV presenter and business coach. He has been running a private practice for many years and has learnt by making lots of mistakes as well as implementing business strategies that have now seen his practice build strongly.
He is a Distinction Graduate of the London College of Hypnosis, a full Member of the British Society of Clinical Hypnosis, and has over the last 10 years been featured widely by the media for his work including BBC Television, ITV, Sky 1 and Sky Living, and national newspapers and online websites including the *Sunday Times* and the *Daily Telegraph*, as well as high street magazines including *Cosmopolitan*, *Grazia*, and *Director*. Prior to starting his own business he was a commercial director before later moving into HR and Training.
He is also a Member of the Chartered Institute of Personnel and Development

the hypnotherapy experts

Andrew Rondeau Andrew is a digital and business consultant and works in partnership with Steve Miller running the Hypnotherapy Business School and Monetise Your Talent businesses. With comprehensive experience of digital marketing Andrew brings his talent and experience to helping clients drive forward their business online.

Sally Coombs Sally became passionate about hypnotherapy after her own experience of its effects.
In the middle of a session she had a light bulb moment, a seed of an idea that quite literally changed her life. She decided to re-focus over 20 years' experience of people-helping work, and to become a hypnotherapist.
From her early work with anxiety and stress Sally became aware of the need for a fertility-focused service.
Sally did specialist training and set up a practice with an acupuncturist specialising in fertility.
Sally offers a complete service promoting fertility, pregnancy and post-natal wellbeing for men and women.

Nicola Beattie specialises in addictions and addictive behaviour, working with cocaine, food and sugar addiction among many others. She uses a combination of EMDR trauma resolving techniques, psychotherapy, coaching techniques and hypnotherapy to help generate new behaviours.
Her six-session Axeing Addiction programme is very successful and includes tailored coaching support between sessions. She uses her personal experience to relate to her clients. Nicola says: "Nowadays, I have what I consider a healthy relationship with my previous addictive habits and have learnt what can trigger my 'addictive side' and how to manage this.
Previously, I worked as an executive in the city and (at the other end of the scale!) I have been a single mother of two on benefits so have experienced life from many angles and take

the hypnotherapy experts

each person as I find them without judgement." Read more about Nicola's programme at www.axeingaddictions.co.uk

Claire McGrath Claire is an anxiety management consultant and runs a busy practice in Gloucestershire. As well as working with private individual clients both face to face and via Skype, she also provides support and workshops for corporates.
One of the UK's top independent mind-programming specialists, Claire is renowned at treating a number of conditions. She specialises in working with anxiety and in particular with executives. She has developed her own mindset coaching programme, which includes cognitive therapy, NLP and clinical hypnotherapy.
She has also worked as a therapist mentor/trainer, helping therapists to achieve levels of excellence in their own consulting rooms.
Claire is a member of the CNHC, the GHR and an advanced member of the International Association of Evidence Based Psychotherapists.
More information about Claire can be found at www.MrsMindset.com

Ann Jaloba is a journalist of over 30 years experience and a practising hypnotherapist. She has developed a niche coaching those in the therapy field and other healthcare areas to write. She is now branching out into publishing self help titles and will be publishing several books in this field next year. You can find out more about Ann at www.annjaloba.com

Philip Ayres As well as being a qualified hypnotherapist, Philip also holds qualifications in Eye Movement Desensitization Reprocessing (E.M.D.R.), and is a Master Practitioner in Neuro Linguistic Programming. A keen flyer he uses his experience of flying light aircraft and microlights to explain the process of flight to his clients as he works to conquer their fear. His Flying Fabulously Toolkit helps clients both before and during their flights and he has many clients who have found a new freedom after sessions with him.

Graham Parish Is The Tinnitus Man, a qualified hypnotherapist and an NLP master practitioner, he has recently become one of the first NLP Master Coach practitioners in the UK. He moved to specialise in the neglected field of tinnitus when his partner developed the condition after a bout of glandular fever. He aims to help people to live in peace with their condition using effective strategies mind coaching and advanced hypnosis techniques to help reduce the constant discomfort of tinnitus. Through more study he has turned himself into an expert on hearing and the workings of the ear so he can fully explain what is happening to his clients.

Dan Regan Dan has been described as 'probably the UK's leading anxiety management hypnotherapist', He runs busy hypnotherapy clinics in Ely, Cambridgeshire and Newmarket, Suffolk, as well as working internationally online.
In 2014, he was awarded the title 'Hypnotherapy Business of the Year' by the renowned Hypnotherapy Business School. Having himself suffered with and overcome anxiety, Dan has a particular interest in helping clients overcome their anxiety, panic attacks and phobias. Many of his success stories appear on his website in the client written and video testimonials published there. More information about Dan can be found at www.danreganhypnotherapy.co.uk

Daniel McDermid Daniel's first career, was that of a professional boxer until early retirement following injury, cut short his dreams of glory. His opponents included current world lightweight champion Terry Flanagan and European titleholder

the hypnotherapy experts

Josh Warrington. He says: "I enjoyed training, but when I quit the ring, I gave up exercise, developed a taste for pizza and piled on the weight – more than four stone in fewer than six months. So I know, how easy it is to pile on the pounds.
I tried to add a bit of weight to my grey matter too and having gained a degree in psychology, I embarked on courses with the London College of Clinical Hypnosis.
Oh, and I also shed all that excess weight I'd stacked up.
I set up my practice: Leeds Hypnotherapy Clinic and have written a book called *Stop Smoking: It's a Doddle*.
I had the good fortune to find inspiration from celebrated weight-loss hypnotherapist Steve Miller who encouraged me to establish this Man Up Lose Weight programme."

Rosalind Smith has successfully helped thousands of people in the UK and internationally to achieve their personal aims.. She says: "Confidence, motivation and self-esteem is included in the support I offer, achieving significant weight loss by managing eating habits.
After struggling with emotional eating problems myself I have a natural empathy of client's experiences which assists in achieving their goals. In 2014 my first book *Your Road To Change* was published along with 8 additional ebooks.
As a qualified, registered Clinical Hypnotherapist and NLP Practitioner I regularly present on the local radio and featured in the press."

Manjit Kaur Ruprai had a long career in mental health services and education, then decided to follow her instincts to train as a Clinical Hypnotherapist. She has a keen interest in helping people to lose weight. She says: "Soon after setting up 'Your Weight Loss Whippet' and working with a diverse clientele, I decided to create the Asian Exclusive Weight Loss Programme as I have a history of chronic illness due to unhealthy eating. I recognised that this was not unusual in the Asian community and decided to change it. I am passionate about this programme as I want to help Asians to slim down and regain control over food through a positive mindset."

Foreword

by Peter Mabbutt

I was very pleased when I was asked to write a foreword to a book whose aim is to help hypnotherapists who want to specialise and become experts in a particular area.

My own experience has been one where working in the niche of pain management and trauma has opened many opportunities and chances to work with new clients and with people from varied professional fields, both in the UK and internationally. It has also enabled me to get involved in projects which are developing hypnotherapy as a serious clinical tool.

Like many of us, I had a different professional background before I became a hypnotherapist. I originally trained in psychopharmacology and for many years I worked as a researcher in this field at Guys and St Thomas teaching hospital in London. My particular interests were anxiety and the effects of dependence on tranquilisers. Like many people who love what they do and are good at their job, I got promoted. And, like many of those people, I ended up being promoted out of the work I had so enjoyed doing. I had always loved dealing with people and had often been told by others, both professionally and in personal life, that I was good at 'giving advice'. This, plus my professional interest in anxiety, meant that talking therapies and hypnotherapy in particular became my future.

I trained with the London College of Clinical Hypnosis (LCCH) and have now been working as a hypnotherapist for more than 20 years.

I am now the CEO/Director at the LCCH and programme leader for the MSc clinical hypnotherapy course. This master's course represents an advance for the profession as it is run in a collaborative partnership with the University of West London and so brings hypnotherapy into the mainstream.

I love this teaching side of my work. It is wonderful to be able to watch and be a part of students learning and developing both the academic and the practical skills to become practising hypnotherapists. I still see clients. I believe very firmly that if you are teaching people how to see clients then you need to be seeing clients yourself.

As I watch the students on the programmes at the LCCH, I often feel I have a good idea of the direction in which they will move and where they are likely to end up as their careers develop. As they begin to learn and practise, they will be drawn to one area which somehow fits with their personality and interests. Steve Miller, who writes a chapter for this book, was one of our students many years back. Right from the beginning, I could tell what he would end up doing and I am not at all surprised to see how successful he is, with all the passion and energy he brings to his field.

At the college, we also run a goal-directed master class and this often provides the arena in which people find their direction. This programme is frequently the way people get that 'kick' to push them to success. Time and again that will involve individuals finding the area they want to be in and often that just seems to happen naturally.

I do believe that specialising in the area you love is good. I also believe that the specialism will often find the person, that is certainly what happened to me.

For myself, if anyone had asked me years back what I would have specialised in, I would have thought that I would have ended up specialising in anxiety and phobias as my background was so strongly in that area and that was what I had done a lot of work around. It did not turn out like that. The path I took was different, and I ended up spending more time on pain management and trauma.

This felt like this just 'sort of happened', which is why I say that the specialism chose me. I was seeing people for a whole variety of conditions in the area of pain and trauma. I was getting good results and those satisfied clients would recommend me to others, so I would see more people with similar conditions. All the time I was learning and developing and getting practical experience in this area and it snowballed from there.

Then, something else happened which can happen if you develop a specialism and a reputation in your chosen area. Opportunities arise and things you didn't anticipate can take off. What happened to me was this: a hospital with which the LCCH was connected in

the hypnotherapy experts

Malaysia wanted me to do a talk; that talk was picked up by the lead of orthopaedic surgery in that hospital, from that things developed into a research project. I was then involved in setting up the hypnotherapy pain management clinic and research programme at the University of Malaya hospital in Kuala Lumpur and I am also the consultant for the hypnotherapy unit at the Panatal Hospital in Kuala Lumpur.

So my interest in pain management has ended up bringing me to the centre of some very interesting developments around how hypnotherapy can help with pain management. I work in various countries, with many professional teams and there are always new directions.

Fairly recently, my special interest in pain management has led to an interesting and valuable sideline of working with hypnosis and childbirth and I have become involved with a university project to train midwives in the use of hypnosis.

This is a great time for hypnotherapy as there is a growing understanding of the mind-body connection. I am very pleased to see that the notion of the mind-body connection is being taken more seriously by both the general public and by medical professionals. We can now see, and there is considerable and robust evidence to show, that an optimistic mindset, a cascade of positive emotions, can protect our immune system. The profession is growing and becoming more professional and I am especially keen on what I would call the ethical side of hypnotherapy. I see this as working with clients to help solve their issues, without the pretence that everything can be put right immediately by some magical process.
I myself am very interested in why the things we use with our clients work. Sometimes there will be a clear evidence base but I am also interested in why things work when we cannot see

that clear evidence base. It is important to work with people's own belief systems and if you are specialising in one area it is possibly easier to do this. Specialists have a lot to offer, even those who are quite controversial can spark us all to think about what we are doing and how we can develop.

One final point, it is worth keeping up with new technology to get the message across. I have been doing this by podcasting twice a month on matters which are of interest of therapists and hypnotherapists in particular. (You can find these on itunes by Googling LCCH podcast). I hope that in the future I will interview the contributors to this book so keep looking in.

The hypnotherapy experts

Introduction

by Ann Jaloba

Welcome to *The Hypnotherapy Experts*, you're going to enjoy this and learn a lot as well. It had been in my mind to put together a book on specialising and developing an expertise in one area for some time now. As with so many of my ideas, the good ones anyway, they begin with practice and especially with my practise as a supervisor.

I was becoming more and more aware from my own supervisees that the ones who were doing the best were the ones who were developing a specialist niche.

They had the highest success rates when it came to seeing clients, and were the happiest and most satisfied with the way their career and businesses were developing. They radiated a quiet confidence and that confidence came from the fact that they knew what they were doing. I got the feeling that anything a client could bring to them they would cope with, they would know what techniques to use, what knowledge to seek out, how to use all this and what to do next. The fact that they are so confident and competent means that they attract clients and get great results. This breeds success; they build a local and even a wider audience.

Thinking about it, it was not surprising that these emerging experts were so happy in their work. People naturally gravitate to areas which interest them so they often started from way out ahead, with an in-depth knowledge of their areas. And they were so keen to learn more and practise more that they stayed enthusiastic. More than one of them told me that often what they did, did not even feel like work. I was reminded of that old saying: 'find something you love doing and you'll never have to work a day in your life'.

I noticed that a number of experts were bringing previous work and life experience into their hypnotherapy niche. So I was supervising teachers who could not take any more in the classroom, but loved working with children, and a health professional who had moved over to specialising in using hypnotherapy for pain management.

Some of the contributors to this book will tell you about how their life experiences, and how they overcame their own blocks, which led them to a specialist niche. It is my firm belief that you will never succeed in this profession unless you are passionate and happy about what you do – clients can very quickly pick up those who don't want to be there.

As a group, our clients are also becoming more demanding. Hypnotherapy is an over-crowded profession and there is more than enough competition out there and our potential clients can easily shop around. If there is any reason why a client with a problem would not choose to come to an expert in that problem, rather than a general hypnotherapist, then I can't think of it. As you become an expert a wider world opens up to you. You can write, even write a book, you can develop a product range. You are an expert and people will pay to hear what you have to say. By specialising you have narrowed the area you have to keep up to date on, so it's much easier to keep on top of everything which comes out in your field. You can provide regular updates on the latest research and developments in your field. You can build networks of other people working in that area and also work with complementary professionals.

It might be as you read this book one specialist niche attracts you. 'I want to do that,' you might say. Or perhaps you will follow the process which some of the contributors to this book have gone through and some up with a brand new niche. Or you could mix and match. Anyone thinking of a slimming programme for Asian men yet? Or how about helping anxious executives in a professional field with which you are very familiar? The one niche can lead to others. I found this in my own journey. I developed a niche, which largely grew out of my supervision work. I started by coaching people to develop a successful therapy career, this lead to me coaching and training therapists how to write and publish (an area in which I have previous expertise) and this has lead to me recently setting up as a publisher in my own right.

You can see other people's journeys of how they became experts as you read this book. All have found their own path, which develops their field of expertise. Sally Coombs suggests that those who work with fertility issues may find it a natural extension to branch out into hypno-birthing. She is currently writing a book on the fertility journey. Manjit Kaur Ruprai, who is already building a very successful business in working with the Asian community for weightloss has not only started writing a book, she is planning to translate it into Punjabi as well. (This will be a learning curve for me as well as I am publishing it!). Then Nicola Beattie, making a very good living working with cocaine addiction, is branching out into an area about which she is even more passionate, helping women who develop addictions in mid-life as they face the challenge of changing life circumstances. She is also writing a book due out next year.

You can find out more about what our contributors are up to as you read their chapters. But what comes across so clearly is how brightly they see their futures and how passionate they are about helping their clients.

I hope you enjoy your journey. Join us and become an A list expert yourself.

Part One

Specialise: the best route to success

Choosing a niche can be the way to turbo-charging your business and leave the generalists behind. In this section hypnotherapist and business guru Steve Miller, who champions this approach, shares his secrets and his associate Andrew Rondeau tells you how to target a market and develop products around your niche.

the hypnotherapy experts

Chapter One

Business brilliance, why you should choose a niche

A crowded market means that it makes sense to become and expert and niche in a specialist area. Business guru and famous hypnotherapist Steve Miller tells you how to do this strategically and develop a service which will ensure you see more clients and make more money

I remember the days when posting an advertisement in the local paper got the phone ringing. Back then students would 'graduate' from their hypnotherapy training schools and find it relatively easy to get clients through their door. Well, let me be honest with you; those days are well and truly over and anyone thinking that a career as a full-time hypnotherapist is an easy ride is thinking foolishly. With more hypnotherapy training schools turning out more hypnotherapists every month, the reality is that the market is saturated, and massively competitive.

Indeed a survey commissioned by the Hypnotherapy Business School found that the average hypnotherapist sees just three clients per week. But you have a talent and you deserve to share your talent. In this chapter I want to support you as you build, develop and elevate your hypnotherapy practice. Yes, it is tougher and you have to work harder at building a business, but can it be done? Too right it can.

The Hope
I do bring good news. I am a positive guy by nature and always believe there is a way. Building a hypnotherapy business is a challenge but yes there are ways! However in a competitive climate you are well advised to think of building your hypnotherapy business *strategically*. Gone are the days where throwing a few leaflets around, dropping off your business cards in doctors' surgeries, and popping an advert in your local rag pulled in the clients.

Indeed you may have yourself been disappointed if placing adverts in newspapers or online has delivered zero results. But don't worry there is a solution.

These days the winners are more strategic in their approach to building their hypnotherapy business; they think about building a brand that rocks, implementing a client engagement strategy that is smart, and delivering a service that builds a great reputation fast.

Yes, there is hope, but sadly many will not make it. Only the smart will make it big and build a practice where they are not constantly desperate for the phone to ring. I want you to think like a winner, believe like a winner and join me in this chapter as I take you on a path to creatively build your own hypnotherapy practice.

You have talent. You deserve to shine. You can make it happen. I will now guide you through my business success strategies to show you how it is done.

I learnt the hard way, and trust me I have made lots of mistakes and wasted lots of money in the building of my hypnotherapy business.

However, I don't look back with regret, because now I can help fellow professionals grow their hypnotherapy business without making the shocking mistakes I once made. I encourage you to embrace the seven strategies I set out here, they are my seven golden rules, and they work.

Strategy 1: Niche
While there is still room for generalists, the busy generalist is dying fast because the hypnotherapy market is saturated. As soon as I mention the word 'niche', many panic at the thought of losing clients with presenting conditions outside of their chosen niche. I encourage you to let go of this fear and rejoice in becoming a renowned expert in your local area, and even further afield, nationally and internationally.

When someone is experiencing an emotional or physical pain they usually want the best; they want the expert who is renowned for his or her knowledge and skill. Because of this, they are usually more attracted to a niche, a specialist, professional. When I first started out it was pretty easy attaining clients for a large range of conditions, but as the years went on it became tougher. I had two choices one of which was to crack on fighting as a generalist or follow the alternative to become renowned as an expert working in one particular field.

Making the latter decision was the best call and I went on to build a hugely successful weightloss practice, establishing myself locally as an expert before taking my work to a national and international level.

You can do the same! Do not underestimate your wealth of knowledge and expertise, and consider following the niche path.

Yes it takes time and yes it will be hard work, but as Henry Ford said, "the harder I work the luckier I become". So here are ten good reasons you should niche as a hypnotherapist.
1. The market is saturated so you therefore need to stand out as an expert.
2. You will be able to command a higher fee for your services if you are a niche practitioner.
3. Marketing and selling your online product portfolio is much easier if you are a niche practitioner.
4. Elevating your public profile is easier because the media often call on experts who represent a specific condition.

5. Attaining a book deal and selling lots of copies is more likely if you niche.
6. Your marketing can be better targeted and you will waste less money marketing your business if you become a niche hypnotherapist.
7. You will have more time to spend enhancing the programme of hypnotherapy you offer clients as you will be focused on one specific condition.
8. You will find it easier to get referrals because people will be clear about what you do.
9. As a niche hypnotherapist you will become unique, therefore you will have less competition.
10. You become a big fish in a small pond.

Strategy 2: Brand Yourself Brilliant
If you want the phone to ring and the emails to come in you will need to build a brand that oozes 'come get me'. To help define and build your brand I encourage you to ask yourself the following questions:

a) Who is my ideal client?
b) What values do I have that I want to share with my ideal client?
c) What personality do I want my hypnotherapy business to have?
d) What business name will represent my brand well?
e) What creative visuals will paint the feelings of my brand?
f) What tangible uniqueness is there around my brand?
g) What colour scheme aligns to my brand?

As you work through those questions collate all the information and begin to define your brand. Here is an example of my very own answers that helped me build the brand for my weightloss hypnotherapy business.
a) My ideal client is female, aged 30 to 60 and she wants to lose weight to feel glamorous and more confident.

b) I value telling it how it is, having motivational flair at the heart of my work and rejoicing in the reality that slim is wonderful.
c) Straight-talking, bold, results-driven, and with humour running through its entity.
d) Your Weight Loss Master.
e) Before and after photographs and associated visuals that represent fun, energy and results.
f) It takes no prisoners, results come first, waffle and excuses are barred.
g) Pink, Pink and even more Pink!

As you build your brand think of it as a person and ensure all your marketing aligns to it. One of the big mistakes is often trying to please everyone with your brand. You can't. Your brand will not appeal to everyone, some will hate it and many will love it, but remember that hated is rated!

You don't want to have a beige brand; you want it to shine, and represent the values you believe in. Of course ensure you have a creative logo designed to represent your brand, but remember your brand is not just about a logo. It is you and the messages you consistently put out there.

Strategy 3: implement website essentials
Unless you want to attract a spiritual client (and yes I do believe in angels), I recommend you steer clear of rainbows and visuals aligned to faith on your website and avoid crystals as well.

Your website needs to ooze personality and be in alignment with your brand and ideal client. Use the following checklist I put together with the help of Adventure Graphics, (a website design company who have developed numerous websites for hypnotherapists, you can find out more about them at www.adventuregraphics.co.uk)

This list will help you develop a website that is more likely to get your phone ringing and your email box filling up.

o *Less Is More:* Visitors to your website want to know what you do, how you do it, proof that you can do it, details of your fees, and how to contact you. Keep your website waffle free and ensure key information is easy to retrieve. A packed website is a real turn off for visitors, so remember to stick to the point rather than adding lots of information that the majority of your visitors just don't have time to read.

o *Make Navigation Simple:* I am a firm believer in ensuring a website is designed with logical navigation. This means having page buttons that do what they say on the tin and tell the visitor what they will find when they click on them, as well as appropriate pop ups and links to pages your visitors will want to find. Think of it like a road map helping someone who is a bit lost; what the person wants is a map that is simple to follow.

o *Use Three Colours Maximum:* You want your site to ooze creativity. In doing so I recommend that you use three colours maximum. Too many colours and it looks messy! Talk to your web designer about what colours will work best.

o *Ensure Headings Are Bold:* Think through the key information your prospective clients want to see. Once you have done this, I recommend that you build the relevant information into key categories and then use a bold heading per category. This will ensure your visitors are able quickly to get the information they need.

o *Use Video and Photos:* The key goal of your website is to sell your products and services. I therefore recommend you use the power of video to get your message across on your website, including video testimonials and videos of yourself. Of course always ensure expressed permission is granted before posting client testimonials. In addition invest in professional photography because your image is massively important.

o *Contact Details:* You would be amazed how many websites make it difficult to make contact. Ensure these are clear and use a contact form to help reduce spam.

Strategy 4: engage with conviction and creativity
Yes, of course it is essential that you have your social media platforms set up; however gone are the days where you could hide behind a Facebook page and hope that your message was loudly received.

Engaging with prospective clients comes in many forms, and there are numerous marketing channels you may use to showcase your talent and get your name out there. Rather than simply offering you an exhaustive list of marketing channels, I will outline the five that I have focused upon to build my hypnotherapy business over the last few years and those which I recommend you follow.

Facebook
I am a Facebook Queen! I love it! Over the last few years I have used Facebook to build my email list, sell my products, and get face-to-face clients. I recommend the following tips to help make Facebook work for you:

a) A business page header that is aligned to your ideal client.
b) Avoid dreary academic posts. Most clients will not be interested in them at all and such posts will probably turn them off.
c) Post practical supportive 'take-out' for your ideal client. Let them see that you are an expert in your field.
d) Use video and showcase your expertise. However make the videos around 90 seconds maximum and be charismatic as you present.
e) Set up a clinic and get your ideal clients engaged. Again this will show them that you know your stuff.
f) Post visuals that are engaging and aim to intrigue prospective clients.
g) Boost your page, but target the audience carefully using the Facebook functions.

h) Post visuals and videos of client testimonials, but remember to seek the clients expressed permission first.

i) Boost posts that are engaging and remember to include a link to your free guide to help build your email list.

j) Sell your message via video and posts in a practical engaging manner that promotes you as a leader in your niche.

Nurture and build your email list

Building an email list is crucial. Those on your list are potential clients so it's important to nurture them so that they 'feel the love'. They are your tribe. By signing up, they have given you their commitment. They trust you with their email address and in return they receive your free guide and they deserve the 'love'.

I recommend you never stop building your list so invest wisely to make it happen month after month. This may include continuous boosting of your Facebook page, boosting posts that include a link to your free giveaway, as well as promoting your free giveaway via Twitter. As you build your list, I recommend you set up a number of automated emails that are sent out weekly to new subscribers. Thereafter you can offer lots of content rich substance to your list including:

a) Emails that contain hints, tips and strategies so that you are supporting those on your list to achieve their goals.

b) Videos of you sharing strategies to help members on your list achieve their goals.

c) Links to your blogs and other associated content you wish to redirect those on your list to read.

d) Offers of your services; however bear in mind that your focus on sales should be restricted, otherwise your fans may unsubscribe *fast*.

e) Updates of human interest that you feel your list may be interested in. This may include trends and current news aligned to your niche.

Bear in mind that you need to ensure the tone of your emails align to your ideal client and your brand.

Use Twitter effectively

It took me some time to work out how to get on top of Twitter and use it to good effect. It is an engagement strategy I encourage you to use, however there is some definite best practice in doing so. Use the following tips to help you take advantage of Twitter:

- Engage with others. Being perceived as an expert on Twitter is the goal and let's face it, you are an expert. You have talent and you should feel confident to showcase it. As you tweet make sure that you tweet content aligned to your niche and get people to recognise that you know what you are talking about. By offering bits of advice for free, people are more likely to take you seriously and do business with you.
- Tweet regularly so that you build up your followers. Ensure all tweets are content rich and think about scheduling your tweets by using Hoot Suite.
- Ask questions. Doing this will help encourage others to engage with you. Questions can also help you do market research for the benefit of your hypnotherapy business.
- You only have a certain number of characters to use on Twitter so if you are copying a link in your tweet consider using something like tinyurl.com which allows you to shorten URL's.
- Retweet loads! To retweet (RT) means that you will be reposting someone else's tweet on your Twitter page. I strongly recommend you do this as it builds the relationship with your own followers and it encourages them to do the same for you. It may also build your follower numbers, some of whom may be very influential.
- Don't keep promoting your business. It may be tempting to be tweeting constantly about your offers and your business, but I

caution you against this. Doing so will just encourage people to stop following you.
- Consider doing a Twitter advertising campaign. Such campaigns help ensure your tweets are targeted to your ideal client.

Generate good PR
As a hypnotherapist you are well placed to generate your own publicity and you only need one appropriate client to generate media exposure for yourself!. Human interest stories are always in demand and you have them.

The good work you do may well receive exposure either in print or online. Of course your client will have to offer you expressed permission to share their story with the media (the media will want to talk to them), and if permission is granted you have a platform to publicise your talent widely.

It is all in the strength of the story, so the more unusual the better. For example, I doubt very much journalists will get excited about a stop smoking story unless there was a jaw dropping angle. However if you have helped someone overcome anxiety and they have left the house for the first time in a year, then that is most definitely newsworthy. If you have a story you feel will capture the interest of the media then follow the steps below to help get it published.

Step 1: Ensure you have discussed PR with your client and attained their consent.
Step 2: Prepare a strong press release that includes quotes, a strong headline and body copy that will engage the interest of a journalist.
Step 3: Contact the media outlet that you believe aligns to your ideal client.
Step 4: Offer your story as an exclusive and explain that you will send over the press release along with high resolution photos.
Step 5: Call back to check the journalist received the press release.

Explain that you will call back in three days' time to see if they want to run the story.
Step 6: After three days call the journalist to see if they want to run the story. If they do then ensure your story remains exclusively for them. If not then thank the journalist and move on to another media provider.
Step 7: Once the story has been run tweet it , share it on Facebook and email it to your list. Then call the journalist to thank them.

Use webinars and teleseminars
Technology rocks for us hypnotherapists. Promoting your talent and pulling in an audience via a complimentary webinar or teleseminar can be well worth doing. It provides an opportunity for you to reach out and increase new faces into your audience, as well as engaging those that are already on your email list. Here are some best practice tips to help ensure your webinar or teleseminar is successful.

a) Creatively promote your webinar or teleseminar for at least two weeks before it takes place. This will help to increase your audience figures.
b) Ensure the webinar or teleseminar has a captivating title and aligns to your business niche.
c) Have a creatively powerful registration page ensuring that you promote the benefits of attending your webinar or teleseminar.
d) If you are doing a webinar ensure the presentation includes details of who you are, why the audience should listen to you, the benefits of the webinar as well as the core content, and if you are selling something at the end, let your audience know it's worth waiting around because you have something special to offer them.
e) For teleseminars use key bullet point notes to help you take the listeners on a logical journey.
f) As you deliver your webinar or teleseminar, ensure you use an

engaging and expressive style of communication. Also be sure to tell stories and give lots of practical examples.
g) Let your audience know that they will be able to ask questions at the end of the webinar or teleseminar.

Strategy 5: embrace the new business model
Over the years the hypnotherapist's business model was dependent upon seeing clients face-to-face, and whilst seeing clients face-to-face remains a core part of making a living, I encourage you to look at a business model that provides you with an opportunity to earn more. The digital age has provided a mountain of opportunity to get our message out there and share the good work we do as hypnotherapists, but it has also delivered an opportunity to monetise your talent online.

As you will read in the next chapter, your opportunity to monetise your talent is greater than it ever has been.

Yes, you can earn money online, but you can also work with clients via Skype as well as face-to-face in your consulting room. The world really is your oyster if you are willing to put the effort in and work hard.

Being business brilliant is about relishing the opportunity to elevate your business online, so that your passive income increases at the same time as seeing clients face-to-face.

Strategy 6: enhance your complimentary consultation
Enhancing the quality of your complimentary consultation is imperative. Offer some version of a 'free' consultation and I encourage you to recognise that this is one of the best sales tools at your disposal. Below are my six complimentary consultation 'elevators'. Follow these and you will enhance your 'free' consultation and encourage prospective clients to work with you.

- *Elevator 1:* Stop using the word 'free'. Instead use the word 'complimentary'.

- *Elevator 2:* Describe on your website what prospective clients will receive by taking up the complimentary consultation. This should include an exploration of the client's condition, an opportunity for the client to understand how hypnosis and hypnotherapy may support them, a complimentary MP3 which includes a taster of your hypnotic style, and a detailed written prescription (I recommend you have this branded with your contact details laid out on it) outlining how best to move forward.
- *Elevator 3:* When talking to your prospective client spend time initially exploring their problem in detail. Empathise where appropriate and listen well.
- *Elevator 4:* Inspire your prospective client, communicating expressively how hypnosis and hypnotherapy can help them. Ensure you inspire the prospective client at this stage, so that they feel confident in you and your proposal to help them. If you feel you cannot assist, then good business practice, as well as clinical ethics, means that you must refer on.
- *Elevator 5:* Show confidence in how you can help and recommend that the client books with you now. If you are selling your services you should remember that a client can often talk themselves out of booking in with you if you tell them to go away and think about it.
- *Elevator 6:* Thank the client for agreeing to book in with you and hand them their programme prescription.

Strategy 7: Deliver A Five Star Service
Marketing your hypnotherapy business is also very much about the experience of your clients. They are your sales force and will either champion you or not.

With rapport in place you are already halfway there, however delivering a service experience for the client that oozes 'added value' is imperative. I recommend you consider implementing the ten following actions to help ensure the experience your clients receive is exclusive rather than budget.

a) Ensure your consulting room is in a professional setting. This should include close attention to the decoration of the room, the fragrance of the room and the quality of the furnishings within it.

b) Offer your clients a tailored MP3 that they can listen to in between sessions to help them achieve their goal. This will take you around an hour so build the fee into your overall price per session.

c) Develop an e-guide for sale online. I recommend you price this at a standard rate, but you offer it to your paying clients as a complimentary tool as part of your overall package.

d) Have an emergency SOS Skype service for clients. Experience tells me that this is rarely taken up, but is something that will definitely help you stand out against your competition.

e) Set up a secret V.I.P group on Facebook for your clients which offers additional support via content you post. Of course membership will be optional; however you will find that some clients will be keen to join it.

f) Offer a text service for your clients where they can update you on a daily basis about their progress. Again, it is rarely used yet it can help some clients and also help you stand out.

g) Send clients a 'well done' card once their programme of support with you has ended. Enclose a few business cards so that they can hand them out to friends who may also benefit from your service.

h) Offer a complimentary follow-up session for your clients, but build this into your overall fee. I recommend you allow the client to take advantage of this on a date of their choice.

i) Set up an email list for your clients and explain that they can sign up for a complimentary guide on self-hypnosis to help maintain the positive work that has been completed. You can then use this list for other purposes such as offering former clients opportunities to attend your seminars or letting them know of your future products.

j) Just be your terrific self. Clients want to feel loved, valued and cared for.

Some final words
Being a hypnotherapist is a massively rewarding job. Sometimes it can bring business conflict because we are passionate about helping people. Building a business and selling our services can often feel awkward; however I encourage you to see you as a therapist who is also an entrepreneur.

You have trained hard, and you have knowledge and a skill bank that deserves financial reward and at the end of the day we all have bills to pay. I encourage you to drive forward your business and to strategise its growth. You deserve a great business and you deserve to elevate it so that you stand out and sell out.

I wish you the very best.

Want to know more?

You can find out more about choosing a niche by visiting

Steve at The Hypnotherapists and Coaches Business

School (www.hypnotherapybusinessschool.co.uk).

Here he offers a complimentary guide to marketing

essentials for hypnotherapists. He also offers one-to-one

coaching and packages to help you develop and market

your hypnotherapy business.

the hypnotherapy experts

Chapter Two

Choosing your niche and then selling products

Monetising your talent can mean you have a constant and growing passive income. Expert in developing such products, Andrew Rondeau takes you through the process from first e-guide to a high-cost, high-value offer

There is one thing to grasp at the beginning. The ultimate way to monetise your talent is finding a target audience and then convincing them to make repeated purchases from you.

An age-old marketing law is this: "It's much easier to sell *more* to existing customers than it is to find new customers to sell to." Your business stands to gain serious momentum when you offer multiple, related offers to your customer base.

So here is a general example, instead of selling a customer a £10 ebook and then looking for the next customer, you could set up a system to offer them a £10 ebook, then a £25 product, then a £297 product and finally a £997 offer. And that all began with a £10 ebook as a foundation.

So the important thing is to get your existing customers to spend *more* money with you. Perhaps you have a dream to earn £100,000 a year, well there is one lesson to learn: the more money each customer spends with you, the fewer customers you'll need to reach that £100,000 per year.

The idea is simple: get your target audience (subscribers to your services and customers who buy from you) to repeatedly spend money with you. Once you have worked to secure a customer or subscriber, why not allow them to spend as much money with you as they are willing?

You can do this while being totally ethical. I'm not suggesting that you exploit your relationship with others and coerce them into purchasing sub-par products or things they don't really need. I'm talking about making products and services available that provide genuine usefulness to those who are in a position to buy from you.

So think about the big, big difference between these two statements:

1) This product is going to change your business forever . . . it's the best product I've seen in months . . . if you don't buy this today, then you're absolutely nuts . . . it's what I consider to be a 'must-have' for anyone who's serious!
2) If you're ready to XYZ, then I've found this product to be very beneficial in my own business. I use it myself and here are the results that I've achieved. I highly recommend it and will even give you a free copy of XYZ if you are one of the first 50 who buy it.

Both are attempting to get the sale. But one is full of hype and the other is reasonable and empathetic to the target audience.

You need to get your target audience to buy from you. And buy again. And again. And again. Despite popular belief, you can do this without being a money-hungry, conscience-less, in-your-face, psychological mind-games coercer!

And if you do this you can be very, very successful. Let's go back to our general example and look at what the next 12 months could look like for you. Firstly, you are going to create 12 e-guides (reports in your area of expertise which you make available on the web). They will be £10 each and you can create one a month.

Your customers will buy the first one and, in time, buy most of the others. So you are already achieving multiple customer purchases. You can also put together package deals so the 12 guides sell for £77, that way you get larger chunks of cash per transaction. Then you can launch a 'high ticket' offer that sells for £297 or more.

Once you do that you are on the way to making a lot of passive income (Yes, that's *you*!) That's how to begin

There is something else though, which is absolutely essential to get right. We need to talk about choosing a market that you want to build your hypnotherapy business around. A market starts with an area such as 'weight loss', 'anxiety' or 'relationships' to name just three. (Later in the book you will see how specialists work and build strong businesses in different areas).

You might look at a target audience's wants: such as 'those wanting to lose weight', 'those wanting to reduce their anxiety' or 'those wanting to have healthy relationships'. Then you will want to create multiple, related products to offer that target audience.

So to begin, you want to determine what market is best for you as you begin creating your products.

Three Simple Rules for choosing a market

Now, for me, I have three simple criteria that I look at in deciding what I want to focus upon. I'd suggest that you do the same in evaluating what market you want to build your business upon.

1) A market accustomed to spending money

If the market isn't accustomed to spending money – and, generally, a *lot* of money, then there's no point in directing any effort towards it. 'College students' isn't a great target audience simply because most of them are broke! On the other hand, 'business leaders' spend a lot of money to improve themselves . . . they certainly would qualify.

2) A market that can be presented with a wide variety of offers
If the market is limited in what you can sell to it, then again there is a red flag. You want to be able to present multiple offers related to the general theme of the target audience you have selected.

Let's take the example of the weightloss market. You can sell a variety of both digital and physical products to this market, including:

Eguides, ebooks, access to membership sites, videos and live events on a wide variety of topics including: nutrition; strength training; cardio exercise; supplements; motivation and more.

Physical products such as vitamins, diet supplements, pre-packaged food items, exercise equipment and similar merchandise.

Coaching, consulting and other services such as nutrition counselling, personal training and similar services.

The point is, the people in this market don't just buy one item and call it a day. Instead, they are receptive to a wide variety of products and services, and many people in the market will buy multiple related products and services over their lifetime. (And, you should be selling a variety of these offers to your existing customers to build your business)

3) A market that you are personally attracted to
If you can find a target audience market that meets points 1 and 2 and one in which you have a strong interest, then you've made your choice.

A personal interest, experience or knowledge of a particular target audience gives you an advantage in many areas of building your business.Taking this into consideration, you now need to pick a market. Now, as you think about what market you'd like to enter, consider these two additional tips:

Tip 1: Choose an evergreen market
This is a market that is relevant today, it was relevant last year, and it will be relevant (and popular) two years from now. This gives

you the opportunity to keep selling to the same market for years to come.

Examples of non-evergreen markets would be creating information around something that's new and likely to fall out of favour, such as a specific marketing opportunity or a controversial diet that has just entered the market.

While the overall markets are evergreen (the business market and the weightloss market), some topics or niche markets are not evergreen.

In summary, ask yourself if the market has been around for a long time . . . and if it's likely to continue to be around for some time to come.

If you need to find out more about evergreen markets, check out Google Trends http://www.google.com/trends/. This site gives you a snapshot look at how popular a topic is over several years. This gives you an indication of whether it's an evergreen topic. But best of all, it also shows you which direction the topic is trending. If you see your topic has been trending upwards for a few years, that's a great sign.

Tip 2: Choose a big and profitable market
In other words, choose a market with a lot of people buying products and services, and a lot of marketers servicing these people. This shows you that the market is big, healthy and profitable.

The way you can determine if a market is big is simply by doing a little research online and offline. Run a search in Amazon as well as Google for the market's main keywords, and then ask yourself these questions: are there local shops and service providers catering to this market?

For example, if you run a search for weight loss, you'll find local gyms, personal trainers, nutritionists, exercise supply stores, vitamin and supplement supply stores and similar commercial enterprises all selling their products and services offline. The reason this is important is because you want to make sure the market is so big that it's not just confined to internet users. Are there plenty of different products and services being sold on the market?

This goes back to my point above that you want to find a market that is receptive to a wide variety of offers. Then ask:

- Is there a lot of competition? This is actually a good thing, as it shows you that the market is healthy
- Are marketers paying to reach this market? Are they placing paid ads in offline publications as well as on websites (such as banner ads or the sponsored listings in search engines)? Again, these are all good signs of a healthy market, as no one spends money if they aren't making back this investment.

You'll want to pick a market where you get a resounding 'yes' to each of the above questions.

Another way to get a sense of the size of the market is to use a keyword tool like WordTracker.com (or even Google's keyword tool). What you do is enter in your market's broad keywords (like 'weight loss'), and the tool will show you how many times that particular keyword is searched.

You're looking for big markets where the big keywords are searched into the six figures every month (that is 100,000 plus). Another way to get a feel for the size of a market is to use Facebook's advertising tools. If you log into Facebook and pretend you're going to set up an ad, Facebook will tell you how many people on their network you'll be able to reach by searching for specific user interests.

Now, once you use all the tips above, it will become fairly clear which markets are big and profitable. Then you need to choose one.

After you've determined to which market you're going to sell your products, it's time to get into the actual process of finding the best topic for your product(s).

How To Find The Perfect Idea For Your Product(s)

Let's look at the number one criteria that I believe will allow you to analyse quickly the state of interest in the market you have chosen and find out what should prove to be a hot topic for your next product.

The first criteria is demand. You should be sure that there is a significant amount of interest in a particular idea before you move forward. Obviously, the more interest there is in a topic, the more likely you'll be able to sell a product on that topic. Now, the questions that I almost always get from people are:

○ How can I judge demand or interest towards a particular idea?
○ How can I find ideas that are in demand?

There are a number of ways to find topics that are of significant demand and interest to your marketplace. Let me share a number of ways you can find topics that are making a splash within your particular market.

Keep an eye out on Clickbank's Marketplace (www.clickbank.com). Products that range in the top five positions within a particular category are usually selling very well. I'll give you a quick hint: they wouldn't be selling well if there wasn't interest. Look for categories in the marketplace that are related to your particular target audience and scan through the top five or six products listed. You're certain to find some great ideas for your next product right there.

Here is an example of what I mean. Put in the broad keyword 'weight loss,' and then take note of the results that show up at the top of the list; these are your most popular products (your bestsellers). You'll likely see books on topics such as getting rid of belly fat, using weight training to get slim and using special kinds of diets to lose weight, such as Paleo diets and vegetarian diets.

In addition to taking note of your bestsellers, you'll also want to look for patterns that indicate a particular topic is popular with the market. An example would be; if you see several similar books on the exact same topic on the first page or so of results, that's a good indicator that the topic is in demand. In the case of weight loss, for example, you might see several books on the topic of getting rid of belly fat.

Scan the best-sellers list as Amazon.com. Do a search at Amazon.com (in the 'books' section) for keywords and phrases that are related to your particular market. (for example, 'weight loss' or 'anxiety' or 'relationships'). You should find a nice list of books ranked in order of popularity. This is another built-in research spot for you and loaded with great ideas for your next product. Then you do the same thing here as you did in the Clickbank marketplace:

1. Pay attention to the bestsellers appearing at the top of your search results.
2. Look for multiple books on the same topic, this demonstrates demand for that topic.

Search in Google to see on what topics your competition has created products. Pay attention to those listed on the first page and those who are advertising in the ads on the right hand side of the screen. These will almost always provide you with numerous ideas for your product.

To get a really good idea of what your prospective competitors are selling, you can search for a range of related keywords. Here is an example: Let's suppose you're looking for weight loss sites. Your broad searches might include:

- Weight loss
- Losing weight
- Losing fat
- Fat loss
- Dieting

You get the idea – expand your search a bit with related keywords, and you'll get a better overview of what your competitors are selling. Look in the market-related forums for hot topics that might lend themselves to ideas on which you can write a eguide. There are forums (also known as message boards) for just about every market imaginable. Look for discussions at these forums for ideas. Specifically, look for topics where there is a *lot* of discussion (that is numerous posted messages and replies). Pay special attention to people who are complaining about problems or limitations, where your products might be able to provide solutions.

Also, take note that some forums have 'keyword clouds' which show you which keywords are most popular on the forum. This too will give you an idea of what topics your market wants to know more about.

To find forums in your market, search for your keywords (such as 'weight loss' or 'lose weight' or 'dieting') alongside forum-related words such as 'forum,' or 'discussion forum' or 'message board'. Examples in the weightloss area might be:

o Dieting forum
o Weight loss message board
o Weight loss discussion

Then look in popular article directories for existing interest. Drop by article banks such as GoArticles.com, or EzineArticles.com and look at articles related to your market for ideas. Pay special attention to the most viewed articles as they are a good indicator of which topics are hot. Also, take note of topics that pop up repeatedly and have high views, as this gives an indication of which topics are most popular. Find offline magazines related to your market. Drop by your favourite bookshop or newsagent (or visit magazines.com) and look at articles for product ideas. In particular, pay attention to the articles appearing on the front cover of these magazines, as those are the topics the publishers expect to garner the most interest. This is another tremendous way to find great ideas, especially because you get the benefit of *their* research. They've invested time in deciding *what* to write about, based on their market's interest. You don't need to do this kind of research . . . simply write about what they are writing about!

Now go through this simple process: ask people on any email lists or client lists you have what topics interest them the most. Take the topic that gets the most mentions and create your product about this. (Who better to give you ideas about what to create than those who are most likely to buy the product upon its completion?) See what's popular on Facebook. This social media platform gives users the ability to set up groups and pages which revolve around specific interests. All you have to do to find them is log into Facebook and run a search for your broad keywords on the upper left side of your screen. From there you can browse the pages and groups to see what they're selling and which topics garner the most 'likes,' 'shares' and discussion.

So, there are some interest indicators that will allow you to judge quickly demand for an idea before you start creating it. By using these simple techniques, you should be able to brainstorm quite a few great ideas for your product. And once you have, let's address the two fundamental aspects for making more sales of your next product . . .

Price And Position
Let's start with pricing. Over and over again, the same question comes up in regards to selling a product: how much should I charge for it? Having created over 75 different special e guides, products, services and other information based materials, I can say with great certainty . . . I'm still no expert at pricing!

There are all kinds of formulas for determining price that we won't go into because most are more confusing than they are useful. Let me sum up what I've learned in nine years online and what I go by in pricing my own materials. There are three simple rules that, to me, govern the amount you should charge for your products.

Rule 1 Your content is the most important factor in determining your price. You can pretty much answer "how much should I charge for it" by answering "how much is it worth?"
Think about it: How much would *you* pay for, say, 10 pages of an eguide? Well, that depends, of course, on what it is about. If it's 10 pages of *How to Mud-wrestle an Angry Crocodile*, then chances are you wouldn't pay much for the eguide. On the other hand, if the 10 pages contained a list of the next 20 winners of the World Cup, the information would be quite valuable to you and the amount you'd spend for it would bear this out.

So you can see that your content is the most important factor in determining your price. The point is this: how much you charge for your next product is going to depend upon how good the product is. Can you deliver the goods?

Rule 2 Your competition's inadequacies help place a premium on your content. If you've got something that works which others don't have, that's going to have a big impact upon the price of (and demand for!) your product. Few people will buy a product on something of interest to them if it's the same old thing they've already read/seen a thousand times before. But, if you can prove that you know some secret, have some special insight, possess some short cut, can point to some advantage that your competition doesn't have, then your product's value just went up a few more notches. What's missing from your competition's products and services that you have in your product? Focus on that and you'll find customers focused on you!

Rule 3 Your customer's expectations, buying habits and desires make the final decision. Ultimately, the right price is in the hands of your potential customers. They make the final decision as to whether or not they are willing to pay a certain price for your product. There are several different factors that influence their buying decisions including:

o What they reasonably expect to receive from your product

○ What they are accustomed to paying for similar offers
○ How much of a desire they have for your product at this time

The good news is you can, to some degree, have influence over all of this. Now, let's say your next product is an e-guide.

As a *very general* rule of thumb, I price my e-guides at around £0.50-£0.75 per page. So a seven-to-15 page guide would be £6.99, a 16-to-20 page guide £9.99 and a 20-to-30 page guide £14.99.

Now, again, if this is privileged information that has a much higher value, certainly your pricing would be different, and higher. But, for most e-guides, this is a good guideline to price by. Unless you have some significant reason to look at a different pricing structure, stick with this one.

Now let's move on to positioning. Without delving too deep into positioning – which could be a rather lengthy discussion in itself – what I want to help you do is to develop what's known as a 'USP' (unique sales proposition). The definition of a USP is: "An intentional, clearly-visible means of separating yourself from others to create a competitive edge. It's what makes you different from others used as an advantage. What it is about you that's better than the rest stated in a way that engages prospects? That's your USP."

Let me tell you a story to illustrate this point to perfection . . . when I married my lovely wife 31 years ago, I had a 28-inch waist and weighed in at 155 pounds. I worked out five days a week and was in good shape.

Something happened during the first 27 years of marriage. I developed a new hobby. It's called "eating." Four years ago, I decided it was time to tone up again. My goal is simple: to get back into the best physical shape of my life. At age 49, it's not going to be as easy as it was back at 22, but then again, I've always liked a good challenge.

I went shopping for exercise equipment. I happened to spot a shelf of exercise balls. You know, the big bright blue balls that you inflate and do various exercises on. Having seen that they can be

selling niche products

useful in toning abdominal muscles (which is where I want to start!), I decided to take a closer look.

Here's what I found: four completely identical bright blue exercise balls. I'm mean the *exact* same size. The *exact* same yellow foot pump to inflate the ball. The *exact* same tube of glue to repair the ball should you decide to take a razor blade and slice it to bits after a few days. Three of the products sold for the *exact* same price of £9.99. The fourth product had an asking price of £14.99.

I immediately decided I would buy the £14.99 version. Why did I spend more money for the exact same product? Here's why . . . product A, B and C all had the standard product name of *Brand A Exercise Ball*, *Brand B Exercise Ball* and *Brand C Exercise Ball*. They all showed basically the same photographs of various exercises and the benefits were all basically the same. Product D was entitled *Awesome Abs Exercise Ball*. And the exercises it showed were all designed to strengthen and tone abdominal muscles. Same "product". Different "focus." Game over.

There are three lessons to learn here . . .

1) You can sell the same product at a higher price than your competition. Forget this nonsense that says you should undercut your competitor in price to be successful. Not true. Lower price doesn't mean greater sales. To the contrary, you can actually *raise your price* and sell more than ever. And here's how. . .

2) "The key to selling at a higher price is *positioning*." It's all about how you *present* your offer. It's all about how you *package* your offer. It's about your *position*. A quarter pound hamburger will cost you £2 at McDonald's. The same quarter pound hamburger will cost you £10 at The Hard Rock Cafe. They bill themselves as offering 'gourmet hamburgers'. What's the difference? Position within the industry.

3) An easy way to position for profits is to focus on a niche. Jack Trout, the leading expert on positioning, has taught me two things about positioning:

a) It's better to be first in your people's mind than better.
b) If you can't be first in their minds in one category create a new category.

That's what *Awesome Abs Exercise Ball* did. It probably wasn't the first exercise ball on the market. But, it's the only exercise ball I've ever seen that is focused on abdominal muscles. It has positioned itself to focus on a *niche* market where it can be *first*.

The bottom line is this: You can *sell more* if you *position* yourself *first* in a *specific niche* market.

Now, what does all of that mean to you and your next product? Let's get personal here and talk about creating your unique sales proposition (USP).

While there are many different aspects of developing a USP, I want to look at the two easiest things you can do to develop your own presence and really separate yourself from your competition in an advantageous way. Focus on a specific *benefit*. And ask the following questions.

1. What is it that you've got which no one else does?
2. Specifically, what about your product makes it special? What's different? What's exclusive?
3. Is it the only product available on the topic?
4. Does it have more ideas than any other product?
5. Have you broken things down into the easiest-to-follow steps?
6. Does it include something that's missing from others?
7. Is it written in a more "user-friendly" language?
8. Does it include significantly helpful screenshots?
9. Do you reveal some little-known fact or secret strategy?
10. Have you produced some staggering results?
11. Is it a completely different approach to the subject?
12. Does it contain the latest information or updated ideas?
13. Does it disclose something that's 'top secret'?
14. Is it the most complete product available?
15. Does it explain things in greater detail?

16. Is it full of ways to apply existing information?
17. Does it have brainstorming exercises?
18. Does it include things like forms and worksheets?
19. Is it specifically for 'advanced users'?
20. Does it expand upon an existing concept?
21. Does it offer an easier or faster way to accomplish a task?
22. Does it offer a different solution to a common problem?

I've just given you more than 20 different ways that your product can be positioned in a unique way. Surely there is something among the questions that I've just asked to which you can respond with an emphatic "yes"!

Listen, you've got something in your product that no one else has and that's what we need to determine. What is it about your product that stands out among what others are offering? Focus on that. Focus on a specific benefit to the reader – what can you offer them that no one else can?

Then there is a second thing you can focus on. This is a specific *crowd*. That is, position your product for a specific demographic group. With this approach, the focus is less on *what* you're teaching in the product and more on *who* you're teaching it to.

You can also focus on a specific crowd in order to position your next product. That's another aspect of what the *Awesome Abs Ball* people did. They focused on a specific group of people: those wanting to tone up their abs. You can do this too, in a couple of specific ways.

Firstly, by experience or skill level. Focus your product based on the experience level of others. In other words, decide if your product is specifically for beginners or specifically for advanced users. Make it clear that you product is specifically for those who've achieved or not achieved a certain level of advancement. Let me refer to a handful of examples.

If you're creating a product about karate, it can be specifically targeted for "3rd degree black belts", for example. That's what makes you different . . . while others might offer resources for *all* students of karate, yours is exclusively for those who've reached a certain level of experience. If you're creating a product about tennis shots, you could focus it specifically on those with a USTA rank of 3.5. I'd be much more likely to buy something related to my skill level than a product for beginners or those who have mastered shots above my skill level.

If you're creating a product about parenting, then you might position it specifically for first-time parents. Again, that makes you different.

If you're creating a product about internet marketing, you might want to focus it on different qualifications of experience such as: for those who are beginners, for those who already have a website, for those without a list, for those who are already making £50,000 a year, etc.

So, that's one way of distinguishing yourself by targeting specific demographic groups based on "experience and skill levels". The second way is by *Distinction.* That is, by focusing on some adjective that describes a group of people. Again, here are some classic examples:

If you're creating a product about "scrapbooking", then you could target it towards Christian scrapbookers with specific points and references of interest to believers in Jesus Christ.

If you're creating a product about fundraising, then you could target it towards church groups or school groups or civic groups or any other distinctive group of people who are interested in raising funds.

If you're creating a product about selling on eBay, you could focus it on baseball card collectors, antique dealers, wholesalers or any other distinctive group of people who might sell items at the online auction giant's website.

If you're creating a product about saving your marriage you could focus it specifically on wives. Or you could be even more selective by targeting stay-at-home wives, career wives or military wives.

selling niche products

The idea is to find a distinctive group of people and target them with your next product. While most of your competition is catering to the masses, you've separated yourself by going after a slightly smaller demographic among the general audience. Your product is specifically for 3rd degree black belts, those who are having trouble losing that last five pounds, beginning internet marketers, Christian business owners, and school groups looking to raise funds. So, that's how you can position your product in order to make it more desirable to your potential customers and create an advantage over your competition.
Answer just two questions:

1. What does my product offer that no one else does?
2. Who would my product be just perfect for?

Obviously, the best option would be to position your product in both ways: by focusing on a specific benefit *and* a specific group, which is what the *Awesome Abs* people did. And, as you have seen using me as an example, it works.

Closing Thoughts
I hope I have given you a lot of useful information. Now the only thing left is for you to take action. I can tell you what to do and how to do it, but I can't make you do it. That's up to you.

I will finish by reminding you of something that I learned back in my school days that has monumentally changed my life...There are only two ways to get to the top of an oak tree.
One is to sit on an acorn and wait.
The other is to start climbing.
See you at the top!

Want to know more?

Andrew is a digital and business consultant and works in partnership with Steve Miller running the Hypnotherapy Business School (www.hypnotherapybusinessschool.co.uk) and Monetise Your Talent (www.monetiseyourtalent.com) businesses. With comprehensive experience of digital marketing, Andrew helps clients drive forward their business online. Andrew also works closely with Steve supporting members to drive forward their online passive income, and offers regular advice to members so that they are able to turn their online efforts into a strong sustainable business. In addition Andrew brings technical expertise and offers a full consultancy service to members looking to improve website technical matters.

.

Part Two

Choosing the best niche area for you

Finding something for which you have a passion, using your personal experience, spotting a gap in the market . . . all these can help lead you to a niche area where you will shine. In this section hypnotherapists who are A listers in their fields describe how they chose their niche and what they do to help clients. There will be something to inspire you here or their experience might spark you to move into an as yet undeveloped niche.

the hypnotherapy experts

Chapter Three

Hypnosis and fertility go naturally together

This area demands expertise and empathy, but is fantastically rewarding as you help people through a life-changing time where the outcome is uncertain. Sally Coombs describes what it is like to specialise in this area

When I am asked what I do and I explain that I work with fertility using hypnosis I am often met with surprise and disbelief as if the two don't go that naturally together.
But in fact they *really do*.
So let me tell you more about this amazing and deeply rewarding area of work in which you can play a small, but not insignificant part in the personal journey of women and men wanting to have children.

What is infertility?
The National Institute for Health and Clinical Excellence (NICE 2013) defines infertility as "a woman of reproductive age who has not conceived after 1 year of unprotected vaginal sexual intercourse".
Infertility is more of a problem than you may realise, probably

because it is very much a private subject rarely spoken about. According to the Infertility Network UK one in six couples face fertility challenges at some stage or another, many of which will be resolved, but for a minority will not.

Infertility is the second most common reason for women aged 20-45 to go to see their GP, pregnancy being the top reason. And the number of women undergoing fertility treatment in the UK has risen significantly in recent years.

Assumptions are often made that infertility is a woman's problem but it is certainly not; infertility affects both men and women.

Infertility can be due to male factors, female factors, a combination of both, or it may be unknown, what is usually called 'unexplained infertility'. Around one third of couples with fertility problems are given no diagnosis.

Primary Infertility is the inability to conceive as defined above. Secondary infertility is when there is an inability to conceive or maintain a pregnancy after at least one successful birth. Perhaps surprisingly, secondary infertility is more common than primary infertility.

What causes infertility?
The causes tend to be either hormone-related, tubal, uterine, cervical, or male-related. Many cases remain unexplained – where there is no identified biological reason for a couple being unable to conceive after one year of unprotected sex.

There are a whole range of physiological causes for infertility, particularly for women, who have a complex reproductive system.

The better known ones for women include:
- Endometriosis – cells that usually line the inside of the uterus grow outside the uterus, for example in the pelvic cavity, causing fallopian tube blockage and cyst formation
- Hormone imbalance – can affect the menstrual cycle, ovulation

and cause repeated spontaneous miscarriages
- Ovulation disorders – absent or incorrect levels of hormones to stimulate ovulation. A certain level of Follicle Stimulating Hormone (FSH) is needed for egg quality
- Pelvic Inflammatory Disease (PID) – scarring and potential blockages caused by infections, such as sexually-transmitted diseases, in the uterus, fallopian tubes or ovaries
- Polycystic Ovarian Syndrome (PCOS) – a hormonal disturbance causing infrequent or absent ovulation, skin problems and difficulties with weight
- Premature Menopause – periods stop before the age of 40, with or without warning, causing the ovaries to stop producing eggs. In these circumstances IVF with donor eggs is needed

Causes of infertility for men include:
- Inadequate semen to maintain and transport the sperm
- Poor Sperm Quality – either abnormal and/or can't swim effectively enough to get to the egg and fertilise it
- The amount of sperm – low sperm count is known as Oligospermia, and Azoospermia is when there is no sperm present

In addition to physiological factors, there are many other issues that can have a bearing on fertility including diet, nutrition, weight, exercise, general, sexual and mental health, stress levels and emotional or psychological factors.

Infertility is very much a feature of modern times, despite huge advances in fertility treatment since the birth of the first test tube baby, Louise Brown in July 1978. It even seems to be on the increase.

Age is a controversial subject when it comes to fertility; overall statistics show nowadays women are having children later. The proportion of women in the UK having their first child at or after 30 has steadily increased since 1975.

There is much debate about the best time to have a baby, with some advocating the earlier the better. The probability of having a baby decreases by 3 to 5 percent a year after the age 30 and even faster after 40. As a woman ages, her egg supply decreases and the remaining eggs age, reducing their reproductive capacity.

Men's ability to produce efficient healthy sperm can also be affected as they get older. So delaying starting a family can have risks for fertility.

Features of modern-day lifestyles can impact negatively on fertility. These include: chronic over-use of alcohol; high caffeine levels; stress; recreational/prescribed drug use; poor diet; body weight issues (being over or underweight); too much or too little exercise; some non-barrier methods of contraception and smoking.

Male smokers, for instance, have a 30 percent higher chance of infertility. Smoking can affect testosterone, important for healthy sperm development. In women smoking can delay conception, increase the risk of miscarriage and affect hormone levels. Alcohol increases the risk of miscarriage in early pregnancy and influences erectile dysfunction.

Nowadays, infertility seems to be more in the public domain. The Infertility Network UK has an annual national campaign to raise awareness about infertility and its impact. And some professionals within the field have been calling for a shift of focus from infertility treatment to prevention with fertility education incorporated within sex education.

So why did I choose to specialise in infertility?
The honest answer is it was something that evolved over time. I didn't finish my qualification in hypnotherapy and immediately decide that I was going to focus on fertility work. In my first years, I worked mainly with anxiety and stress and from this work it was evident that many women were anxious about their fertility and about becoming pregnant after experiencing miscarriage. There seemed to be a need in this area which got me thinking.

Initially I ruled myself out, after all I didn't have children of my own, but after considering it more deeply I realised that I'd been on my own personal journey: a miscarriage in my thirties, the breakdown of a long-term relationship rocked by this loss, yearning for a child, facing and accepting my childlessness, and being a step-parent.

So having reached a decision, I invested in specialist training (there is a list of courses at the end of this chapter) and obtained the NCHP Certified Hypnotic Fertility Practitioner qualification.

I subsequently set up my own practice with an acupuncturist who also specialises in working with infertility, so that we can offer the combination of our therapies.

I love the variety of work that comes under the umbrella of infertility, and seeing individuals grow through the experience of having therapy. Having a passion for this area of work and empathy for the issues is crucial.

So too is an understanding of the mind-body connection when it comes to fertility. I am a firm believer in the importance of working holistically with fertility issues. In my opinion modern infertility treatments focus too much on the medical and physiological aspects of fertility and consequently over-use IVF.

A purely medical approach views infertility as a biological problem due to the body not functioning properly. A holistic approach takes into account the whole individual, including their emotions and their mind, and the inter-connection between the two. Balance is a key concept to fertility and an inner imbalance can disrupt conception and pregnancy.

And this is where hypnotherapy can play such an important role in assisting fertility.

How hypnotherapy can help with infertility
Although the mind is not the only factor when it comes to fertility, the mind-body connection is a powerful one and research indicates that reproduction is likely to be affected by

the mind. There is a range of research in relation to the use of mind-body approaches with infertility, most notably by Dr Alice Domar, an American psychologist and fertility expert whose pioneering work is described in her book *Conquering Infertility* published in 2002.

The Harvard Behavioral Medicine program for infertility was first started in 1987 in Boston, based on the work of Dr Domar, and Jon Kabatt Zinn, professor of medicine at the University of Massachusetts Medical School. The programme uses mind-body techniques such as hypnosis.

Studies conducted at Harvard Medical School published in the *Journal of the American Medical Women's Association* (1999) and the *Journal of Fertility and Sterility* (2000) were based on 184 women who had been trying to conceive for one to two years.

They were randomly allocated to a 10-week group using mind/body techniques, a 10-week support group, or a routine care control group. In the one-year follow-up period the birth rates for those in the mind/body group were 55 percent, 54 percent for the support group and 20 percent in the control group. The women in the mind/body group also reported greater psychological improvements than the support and control groups. 42 percent of the women in the mind-body group conceived naturally, more than in the control group (20 percent) and the support group (11 percent).

Four other published studies were based on several hundred women with long-term infertility. Of these 42 percent conceived within six months of completing this programme and had significant decreases in psychological symptoms.

With regards to medically assisted reproduction, Professor Levita's research into hypnosis and IVF published in the *Journal of Fertility and Sterility* (2004) is well known. It demonstrated that hypnosis doubled the IVF success rate. His study of 185 women in Soroka Hospital in Israel found 28 percent of women who were hypnotised became pregnant, in comparison to 14 percent of those who were not. Hypnosis was used during the most stressful part of

IVF, at the point of embryo transfer. Hypnosis was found to be far more effective than tranquillisers.

Specifically in relation to female fertility, research reported in the *Journal of Psychosomatic Obstetrics and Gynecology* (2015) looked at the impact of negative childhood experiences on fertility. The study was based on 774 women of reproductive age, 195 of who were pregnant. The researchers explored their hypothesis that negative childhood experiences can result in menstrual cycle irregularities, and related it to their 'life-history theory'; balancing the preservation of one's health as well as the production of offspring that will survive to reproduce themselves. They theorised that: "early life stressors may predispose an individual to adaptively suppress fertility when situations are less than optimal, leading to periods of fertility difficulties even following previous births." The research concluded women who had experienced adverse childhood experiences such as abuse, neglect, household dysfunction and parental substance abuse were more likely to face fertility difficulties, abnormal absences of menstruation lasting three months or more, and taking a longer time to get pregnant.

These new findings aren't about hypnosis, but they highlight the relevance of stressful childhood experiences to fertility, and hypnotherapy has the ability to help resolve the impact of such experiences.

Hypnotherapy and infertility: At what point are you likely to be consulted?

The answer is at any point, and hence there is a need for a flexible, individualised approach to working with infertility.

It is also important to take into account the wider picture. You may be working with a client who has approached you for hypnotherapy as a stand-alone therapy to assist natural conception, for example. Or you may be working alongside other complementary support such as acupuncture, or as a complement to medically-assisted conception.

Managing client expectations
With any fertility work pregnancy can't and shouldn't be guaranteed. It's more about helping the individual to be in the best physical, emotional and psychological state to be able to conceive, to improve their chances and quality of life overall.

Within this scope you may be working on many different levels, helping clients to regain a sense of control, teaching positive coping strategies, facilitating healing and personal growth, resolving past traumas, or promoting relaxation.

Stress can have a significant impact on both male and female fertility, whether this stress is generated by negative thinking or an unhealthy emotion, such as anxiety.

A delicate balance of hormones is needed for reproduction. Stress upsets this fine balance interfering with ovulation, implantation and healthy sperm production. The body goes into survival mode and, as reproduction isn't needed for this, the reproductive system is effectively frozen.

Struggling to conceive over a period of time and going through medical procedures can cause huge stress, strain relationships and finances, and stir up a whole host of emotions including anger, desperation, frustration, grief, jealousy, and insecurity. And then there's the endless waiting for appointments, investigations, results and difficult decisions. All of this can lead to a profound sense of helplessness and inadequacy.

Stress is a key area to work with and relaxation is the foundation to Domar's (2002) work with infertility, as described in *Conquering Infertility*.

Hypnotherapy is a powerful way to reduce anxiety and stress and increase feelings of calmness and confidence. Rebalancing the mind through relaxation methods can promote the body's natural processes, restoring the parasympathetic nervous system affected by chronic stress, stimulating the relaxation response and a return to hormonal balance. This is essential for both natural and medically assisted reproduction.

Specifically with IVF, relaxation and stress reduction techniques are very important for the whole cycle including the two-week period after embryo transfer, as this can be the most anxiety producing time of the process.

With huge levels of stress building up over time in relation to infertility there is a risk of depression and this is something of which you should be mindful when working with clients. Depression can affect male and female fertility, but depression can also be triggered by fertility difficulties and the associated isolation and desperation experienced by some.

Domar's research shows a link between depression and infertility. It indicates infertile women are more depressed than fertile women, depression levels peak two to three years after women start trying to conceive, and infertility has a greater psychological impact than terminal illness.

Some lifestyle changes are favourable to conception, but many people struggle to make these on their own. Here hypnotherapy can help improve many aspects of health and wellbeing by facilitating smoking cessation, healthy weight management, improved sleep, and reduced alcohol consumption.

Experiencing fertility difficulties can seriously impact on confidence, self-esteem and identity and lead to feelings of being overwhelmed, fear, loss and lack of control. Hypnotherapy can support clients with the emotional impact of infertility by helping them to connect to and make use of inner resources such as calmness, confidence and self-belief. Hypnosis can also work cognitively to identify and eliminate negative thinking which drives anxiety, or limiting beliefs not aligned to conception, and re-programme healthier patterns of thinking.

There are a range of physiological causes for infertility in men and women. Hypnotherapy can be used to enhance fertility through self-healing, restoring balance and alleviating physical symptoms. It helps with overcoming fears or phobias which may impact on treatment, such as fear of needles and injections. It can also help clients to prepare physically and emotionally for medical treatments, including IVF, through relaxation and visualisation of positive outcomes such as a nurturing, welcoming womb or healthy embryo development.

Infertility can impact enormously on relationships between a couple, creating emotional strain and conflict as well as pressure on their sexual relationship. For men their sense of masculinity can be affected when there are problems with their sperm. Differences in communication and responses to emotional issues within a relationship can become even more polarised in relation to the pressures of trying to conceive. Sex can become obsessional and functional; focused on making a baby. Frequent and enjoyable sex is important for male and female fertility and therefore reproduction. Extended family relationships and friendships can also be affected, leading to isolation. Hypnosis can help with a range of issues including self-worth, communication and recapturing of sexual intimacy.

Dealing with inner blocks and conflicts can also be helped by hypnosis, which offers a range of techniques to access the unconscious mind in order to resolve past experiences or unconscious issues that may be preventing conception. Examples include childhood abuse, rape, a previous termination, a stillbirth or neonatal death, or adoption. The study into adverse childhood experiences reported in the *Journal of Psychosomatic Obstetrics and Gynecology* (2015) highlights the impact of negative childhood experiences for fertility.

Hypnosis can be used to complement the IVF cycle as relaxation and positive visualisation of the body working well at each stage of IVF can help to increase its effectiveness, I give an example of this in one of my case studies on this book's website (www.myhypnotherapyniche.com). In vitro fertilisation (IVF) is a medically-assisted fertility treatment whereby egg cells are fertilised by sperm outside the woman's body. The long protocol used for IVF involves several different stages. It starts with the de-regulation stage about seven days before a woman's expected period and involves taking medication to suppress normal hormone production, then a further two weeks of follicle stimulating hormone drugs by injection to stimulate the production of several eggs rather than a single egg, and the injection of a hormone called human chorionic gonadotrophin (HCG) to encourage the eggs to mature. The eggs are then harvested from the woman's ovaries, the egg collection stage. The eggs are combined with sperm in a laboratory dish for fertilisation. The best quality embryo or embryos are transferred to the woman's uterus. Two weeks after embryo transfer the women has a pregnancy test. This whole procedure can vary depend on the couple's needs, and whether egg, sperm or embryo donation is involved.

Clients can be helped using a whole range of therapies in addition to hypnosis including the rewind technique, gestalt chair, EFT, parts therapy, coaching, NLP, teaching self-help and relaxation techniques.

My own recommendations
Reflecting on my own journey these are my thoughts about doing fertility-related work.

Doing specialist training in this field has been invaluable, firstly for understanding the mind-body connection in relation to the reproductive system, and the different physiological conditions affecting fertility, and the range of ways in which you can work within this field. I recommend doing specialist training if you are serious about developing this into a niche area.

The whole area of fertility is an ever-changing one so it's important to keep up-to-date with developments.

Having good support and supervision for you is also crucial. Doing this kind of work is hugely rewarding, but it can also be an emotional rollercoaster, especially when working with people going through IVF which can falter at any point along the process, and pregnancy doesn't always result in a happy outcome. I have worked with women through a successful IVF process, but the pregnancy has been followed by a miscarriage and all the heartache that goes with this.

You also need to be confident about your own abilities as well as knowing your own limitations. Often people come for therapy wanting to focus on a solution to their infertility and can be impatient for results or lack awareness about the importance of working with the related issues contributing to infertility.

If you decide to specialise in fertility work there are many opportunities within this niche, for example specialising in male infertility, female infertility, natural fertility, or as a complement to IVF. Or you could develop a complementary niche to fertility and work with pregnancy, or hypno-birthing or post natal issues in order to offer a complete service.

Working with clients: client sessions
I don't have a standard way of working with fertility, a flexible, individualised and person-centred approach is needed.

Key to your work is a thorough intake session, the importance of rapport building and being able to adapt to the client's needs.

You may be approached for a fertility-focused service at any stage of a client's fertility journey – to improve the chances of a natural conception, before seeking medical attention or once physiological issues have been identified. A client may wish to see you in the circumstances of unexplained infertility, prior to the start of IVF, in the middle of IVF, or at the point of embryo transfer during IVF . . . are just some examples.

You may be working predominantly with women, as I do, you may choose to specialise in male fertility, and you may at times consider it appropriate to work with a couple together to address relationship issues. Sometimes my work involves a single session and other times it's much more complex and multi-faceted. Here

hypnosis and fertility

I'm going to concentrate on the assessment session and what areas to cover as this will help determine the focus of other sessions.

Initial session
During your initial session it is important to get a thorough case history which includes discussion about the following areas depending on whether your client is female or male:

- The individual's fertility journey so far – how long they have been trying for a baby, what medical tests and investigations have been done, diagnosis given
- Previous pregnancies/children
- Miscarriage, stillbirth, neo-natal death, termination
- Health history – past problems including sexual and mental health
- Current health –weight/diet, exercise, sleep, alcohol/drugs, stress levels, smoking, medication, menstrual health
- Family history/fertility issues
- Personal history/significant life events
- Sexuality
- Key relationships
- Support network
- Work
- Involvement of other healthcare professionals

Solution-Focused Questions:
As well as gathering this information during the first session I use solution-focused questions to:
- Identify the client's goals for therapy and changes they are seeking to make
- Explore factors affecting the client's current health and wellbeing
- Identify unresolved issues that may be preventing pregnancy

Here are some examples of questions to establish the client's solutions:
- How would you know if these sessions were being useful to you?
- What would be different?
- What changes would we be making together?
- What would you be feeling, thinking, and doing differently that would tell you that things were changing in a positive way?

It also helps to clarify what represents fertility and wellbeing to the client, so I ask questions such as:
- How will you know when you are in a fertile state? What would be different?
- Describe what optimum health and wellbeing means to you? How would you know you have it?
- On a scale of 0 -10, with 10 representing when you are emotionally, mentally and physically balanced, what number represents where you are now? What needs to happen for you to get to 10? What would we work with first?
- If we could work on one thing today to enhance your fertility, what would it be?
- When you are feeling more relaxed, how does your body and mind show this?
- What else will you notice?

Then I will try to explore potential blocks to pregnancy:
- What do you feel is affecting your ability to have a baby?
- What do you think will help you to have a baby?
- What things are you already doing?
- When you think about pregnancy, birth or parenthood is there anything you are worried or concerned about?

I am also listening throughout this session for the emotions and thought processes that the individual describes, as this can provide a helpful insight into the mindset and emotional world of the client.

hypnosis and fertility

I include an introductory hypnosis as part of this session usually to work generally on relaxation and helping the individual to release the negative emotions that may have come up through the talking part of the first session, and to help them connect with positive resources such as balance, calmness and confidence.

Follow-up sessions:
From this initial session you can plan follow up sessions to address the particular needs of the client.

In her book *The Fertile Body Method* Hugo (2009) describes a step-by step approach with six different stages of therapy. I find this a useful guide:

1) Outcome - the assessment, taking a case history, establishing the outcomes desired by the client, using this information to devise a therapy plan

2) Balance – working with the client's mental, emotional and physical state to restore balance and wellbeing. This may include reducing anxiety and stress, negative thinking, and developing positive inner resources

3) Resolve – once the client's wellbeing has improved, addressing unresolved issues that may be preventing conception – for example fears, conflict, past trauma, childhood issues, or unresolved grief

4) Enhance – use of positive visualisation and guided imagery to enhance fertility and the body working well

5) Prepare – mental, emotional and physical preparation for IVF, pregnancy, birth or parenthood

6) Support – support whatever the outcome, for example if conception doesn't happen, to support pregnancy, loss following miscarriage, or coming to terms with not having children, or considering alternatives routes to parenthood

This is a useful therapeutic framework for assisting a client through the process of change and an example is shown in my second case study. This framework is a guideline only to be adapted as needed rather than being a rigid way of working.

And it is not necessarily appropriate in all cases, as you can see from my first case study on the website.

Also your approach will depend on the point that a client contacts you. For example, if a client consults with you whilst in the middle of IVF, it would not be appropriate to be doing resolving work on unconscious blocks. Your focus would be working on what's going to complement and support the effectiveness of IVF and what her needs are at that particular point.

In addition to a well-formulated action plan this needs to be implemented with respect, empathy, sensitivity, non-judgment, and flexibility in order to create a trusting, respectful therapeutic relationship. An empowering approach facilitates the client, and promotes insight, learning and responsibility for change.

Fertility-related technique

If you are going to specialise in fertility work *The Fertile Body Method* by Sjanie Hugo (2009) is a comprehensive resource with a wide variety of scripts relevant for fertility work, and there are many other books focused on mind-body approaches for infertility.

On the website (www.yourhypnotherapyniche.com) you can find a script I have written for pregnancy loss. It may seem somewhat illogical to include this within a chapter on fertility, but in my experience, fertility work often involves helping individuals to grieve and come to terms with previous losses before they feel ready to move on.

Also a positive outcome in terms of pregnancy doesn't guarantee a child, and some pregnancies aren't sustained.

A different approach may be needed if the grief is particularly complex or has got stuck at a particular stage of the grief process – denial, anger, depression, acceptance.

I hope you have found this introduction useful. If you want to read further or undertake training I have included references and information below.

References

NICE (2013, P.9) *Fertility: assessment and treatment for people with fertility problems.* London: NICE, Clinical Guideline 156

DOMAR, A. (2002) *Conquering Infertility.* London: Penguin Books Ltd

Journal of the American Medical Women's Association 1999

Journal of Fertility and Sterility 2000

Journal of Fertility and Sterility 2004

Marni B. Jacobs et al. *'Adverse Childhood Event Experiences, Fertility Difficulties and Menstrual Cycle Characteristics',* Journal of Psychosomatic Obstetrics and Gynecology 2015

HUGO, S. (2009) *The Fertile Body Method.* Carmarthen: Crown House Publishing Ltd

Some Examples of Specialist Training:

'Hypnosis for Fertility' Practitioners Specialist Certification Course training with Sharon Mustard can be found at: http://www.easibirthingtraining.co.uk, this training is independently accredited by the National College of Hypnosis and Psychotherapy (NCHP)

Sjanie Hugo's training:

http://www.thefertilebody.com/events/Details/Fertile_Body_Method_Online_Training_Programme

Russell Davis also does an online fertility CPD course for members of the National Council for Hypnotherapy (NCH), and he runs webinars on fertility for the Infertility Network UK as well as doing his own private work

http://www.thefertilemind.net/

Want to know more?

You can find out more about Sally's fertility services at www.innermindtherapies.co.uk. Sally is currently writing a book to help people through all stages of the fertility journey. This will be out next year. If you would like more information or to pre-order this book email annjaloba@btinternet.com You can download a script based on Sally's approaches and see her cases studies by visiting www.yourhypnotherapyniche.com

Chapter Four

Axeing addictions by breaking the addictive cycle

Nicola Beattie is an expert in helping people break with addictions. She knows that addiction can frequently move from one substance to another so she works to get to the root of the problem

An addiction is a compulsive habit that has become harmful to the user. As a species, we naturally seek pleasurable experiences and experimentation. In fact, alcohol and recreational drugs are used by a majority of young adults, yet only a handful will go on to having a full-blown addiction.

Addictions can be to substances, but it is more likely that we become addicted to the experience we are having, rather than the actual substance itself. In fact, many people with 'addictive personalities' will often jump from one addiction to another. Addictions can range from tobacco, alcohol, narcotics, prescription medications, sex, gambling and shopping (to name just a few). If the experience is fulfilling a need that is lacking in that person's life, it is entirely possible to become addicted to anything.

So how do we differentiate an addiction from a habit? In short, if the habit is causing a negative, long-term impact on yourself and those around you then it's likely to be an addiction.

It is unhelpful in my option to label people as 'addicts' or 'alcoholics' as that implies that their addiction is stronger than they are. This is not an empowering stance from which to make change. I dislike the notion that addiction is a 'disease', in fact I would reject it entirely.

An 'addiction gene' has never been proven to exist, and to take one group, the children of alcoholics are no more likely than anyone else to develop an addiction to alcohol. Attitudes towards (for example) alcohol, can vary massively between cultures, which is why certain nationalities and ethnicities have more of an issue with this addiction than others.

Remember that it is the *experience* that people can get addicted to, rather than the *substance*. This fact allows the client to make changes to behaviour, without resorting to extreme measures such as abstinence, which can in turn provoke 'black and white' (or 'all or nothing') thinking.

This thinking can itself create obsession and therefore addiction. (I have met clients that have become addicted to their AA meetings and unable to sustain a healthy lifestyle!) Addiction occurs when key areas of life are not being addressed and the lifestyle is not balanced. These key areas are human needs, such as the need to be loved, respected, and empowered. Then there are the needs to be developed creatively, live in a stable environment, make autonomous decisions and be safe from physical and emotional harm. If any of these areas is severely low, then a pleasurable habit can begin to be used to fulfil the need that is lacking.

When changes are made to address this, the addiction can subside as the void that it is trying to fulfil is no longer there. Our human survival instinct is to always push ourselves to develop new skills and interests, without new challenges in place we are much more likely to enter into addictive cycles of behaviour. It is interesting that these behaviours often change over time, while the addiction remains.

The underlying need for the artificial high remains even though the superficial behaviour might change. This underlying need is what we need to address.

Most people enjoy some kind of vice; be it that glass of wine in the evening, occasional cigarette, guilty shopping spree, a flutter on the races or that cheeky 'livener' on a night out. So when do these pleasures stop being a pleasure and become problematic? The truth is genuinely happy people have fewer addictions. The excitement that we get when we want to do something is produced by dopamine, a natural brain chemical (very like cocaine in its effect). This raises our emotional levels so that we want to take action. The warm feelings of satisfaction we get after doing something; eating, laughing, having sex, or achieving some new understanding or skill are produced by endorphin, another natural substance (which is similar to heroin).

Working together, these chemicals keep us interested in doing the biological functions that preserve the human species, and stretch each one of us to learn and achieve.

My work is based on the belief that addictions can be beaten. Addiction can be overcome without a person necessarily becoming dependent on a recovery group and without having to consider themselves as an 'addict' for the rest of their life. To get away from addictive behaviour it is necessary to understand two things: the way these reward mechanisms work, and the way life should be lived in order to receive the natural highs that make addictive activities less attractive. In a well-balanced life, a reasonable amount of natural reward is felt by each human being every day, but in a life where essential emotional needs are not met and abilities are not stretched, the rewards do not come and life feels flat and meaningless.

This kind of life is rich territory for addictions to target, as every addictive substance or behaviour either stimulates a reward mechanism or provides a chemical reward directly.

The addictive cycle
It is useful to understand which parts of the brain are involved in fuelling the addictive cycle. I explain these to clients, giving them nicknames so they understand what is happening. The important parts of the brain in addictive behaviour are:

- The dorsolateral prefrontal cortex - the main decision making part of the brain. Nicknamed *'The CEO'*
- The anterior cingulate - responsible for unconscious processes and keeping the body running smoothly. Nicknamed *'The PA '*
- The amygdala - controls fight or flight impulses. Nicknamed *'The Security Guard'*
- 'The hippocampus - where memories are stored. Nicknamed *'The Library'.*

(You can download a diagram, 'The Brain and the Addictive Cycle' which shows all this at the extras section of this book's website).

So, what typically tends to happen when a client wants to stop the addiction? I explain this to clients using the metaphor of a memo going around the office. So first thing in the morning:

- *'The CEO'* makes a key decision (for example, to stop smoking)
- *'The CEO'* contacts his *'PA'* with the message 'no more smoking'
- *'The PA'* then sends this as a message to the other parts of the brain. To add importance, *'The PA'* tags the message with the chemical dopamine to add urgency

Then around mid-morning, the chemical changes in the brain will start to adjust, this alarms the amygdala (this part of the brain is *'The Security Guard'.* If the level of for example cortisol (stress hormone) is increased or nicotine (from tobacco) is decreased, this part of the brain will begin to investigate).

To do this, *'The Security Guard'* (amygdala) will begin to flag up messages to *'The PA'.* At first *'The PA'* will ignore the messages until the level of dopamine, which is increasing all the time to get

axeing addictions

attention, reaches a critical level. Once the dopamine has reached a certain level, *'The PA'* will investigate the use of (cortisol) and (nicotine) in the body. To do this:

- *'The PA'* references *'The Library'*.
- *'The PA'* will ask *'The Library'* to show examples of when the client has used (nicotine) to relieve stress. Normally *'The Library'* will reference daily examples, showing when (smoking) has been useful to the client
- *'The PA'* bypasses *'The CEO'* and sends a message to *'The Security Guard'*, okaying the use of nicotine to relieve stress (or whatever the client believes their smoking habit is useful to relieve). And so the addictive cycle continues

Changing the books in the library
I talk to the client about 'changing the books in the library'. When changing the cycle of addiction, the anterior cingulate will reference the hippocampus to see when the client has previously used the addictive behaviour to their advantage. So we can see from this example, that 'changing the books' in the library, is vital for long-term change of the addictive habit.

In therapeutic terms, we create new references and memories by accessing negative and repressed instances of when the addictive habit was used in the past, both real and imaginary. If the hippocampus is only referencing positive states, then the negative behaviour will continue. The ultimate aim of the hypnosis will be to access as many uncomfortable, repulsive and revolting states as possible so that in future occurrences, the client will be accessing negative unconscious memories rather than positive ones.

Explaining this process to the client (and drawing it as a diagram) will help them to understand why the addictive behaviour has been continuing up until now, despite their best intentions to make changes.

To change an addictive habit, we need the client to gain a new insight into their addictive behaviour which will in turn, allow them to generate change. Ultimately, happier people have fewer addictions. Checking through this list, you can notice where the gaps are. My addiction plan works by boosting happiness as well as creating revulsion to the old addiction.

Mind and body are inextricably linked, so I encourage clients to take time each day to exercise, and to use self hypnosis or enjoy quiet time to reflect, I encourage them to choose to nourish their body with fresh, clean foods that make them feel good.

Without a client taking action they aren't going anywhere! So I get them to draw up a goals list and set daily and weekly tasks and goals. I also encourage the client to forgive and let it go - the only person who is hurt by old resentments is them. I explain to the client that bearing grudges is toxic and will eat up energies like a cancer. I spend time in sessions helping the client understand and accept that the past is the past and the only person keeping it alive is them.

Everyone is human. We all make mistakes and learning to accept ourselves as well as others for who they are lessens the pressure to attain perfection.

I tell clients: train yourself to focus on the things that you can influence; when you stop worrying about all the things you can't control and focus instead on what you can influence, this will allow you to get the life that you choose.

Focus on the good; actively change persistent negative thinking habits by making the time at the end of each day to consider what three things went well for you. When 'life happens', allow yourself to fully express the feelings; sadness, pain, frustration, happiness . . . don't bottle it up! Really feel the emotion.

And when you're done, move on and feel better. Many people use their addiction as an outlet for emotions. By allowing yourself freedom to express them, this will help break the cycle. Choose happiness! Avoid the trap of reading the news and viewing depressing documentaries or violent movies and instead make better choices about how to spend your precious time doing the things that you enjoy and make you feel good instead. After all, is the best way really to relax, to watch or hear about other people suffering? Persist! Rome wasn't built in a day so learn to accept the bad days as merely blips to overcome. Choose your friends wisely: laughter really can be the best medicine.

My treatment programme
The success of the programme lies in getting the client to see their addiction for what it really is; a drain on their health, finances, time and resources. Many people are blind to what their addiction is actually doing to them. The aim of treatment is to create revulsion to the habit, whilst boosting confidence, teaching coping skills and helping the client develop a realistic overview of their life and lifestyle. I work with the client to set goals to achieve this.

A typical treatment plan for addiction is held over six sessions. The first four are held weekly and then I space the remaining two out over a five-week period. I offer top-up or additional sessions if needed. My clients appreciate that I am accessible to them for further support if needed. My sessions are usually 90 minutes long, however clients can extend the programme if they prefer to work in 60-minute time slots.

Session 1: information
In this session, I take information about the client's medical and emotional background as well as giving a detailed pre-talk on using hypnosis. The client will complete and sign a registration form and give consent for treatment.

I use a client history questionnaire that I complete verbally with the client by talking to them in an informal conversational style. This contains questions such as:

o If my pen was a wand, and I was to wave it, and all would be

just how you wanted it to be, what would be different? (This builds positive expectation, helpful in generating the shift from current to new behaviour).
- Give me a snapshot of your life? If you could change anything, what would that be?
- What do you do for a living? Do you enjoy it?
- If you could change just one thing about yourself what would that be?
- How is your health? (Discuss illnesses or health conditions as physical ailments often give a clue to the types of thought patterns occurring)
- Do you like where you live?
- Have you a significant other, if so how is the relationship?
- Describe briefly your childhood?
- Is there anything else that I haven't asked you, which might be helpful for me to know?

Recording a short initial support audio can be very useful at this stage, I usually include a passive progressive relaxation because high anxiety levels will often be a contributing factor towards addictive behaviour.

Including an aversion technique towards the addictive behaviour can be a key way to induce the feeling of revulsion and the use of a positive mental rehearsal begins to set the theme for change. Ideally the support audio should be 15-20 minutes in length.

Session 2: creating behaviour change
I begin this session by reviewing the past week. I ask the client: "what is different since last week?" "What were your thoughts at the close of the previous session?" This is usually a good basis to start exploring the client's key beliefs about themselves and their addiction. Also they learn what triggers in the past have led to their current behaviour.

This session introduces the concept of lifestyle analysis and goal-setting tools. These tools help to identify which of the client's needs aren't being currently being met. The resulting goals should be referenced for homework and as an ongoing basis throughout the programme.

It is key to empower the client to make actual changes (or work towards them) during the treatment plan.

Techniques that are helpful in this session include: a wheel of life sheet; a goals sheet and a 6-step-reframe technique I ask clients to aim for 10 goals depending on the outcome of their wheel of life sheet.

These should be short, mid and long-term goals. I use hypnosis as part of the session, teaching self-hypnosis and using the idea of a safe or relaxed place. I also use the 6-step-reframe technique and positive mental rehearsal to follow. I give homework in the form of self-hypnosis or an audio and a goals sheet.

Six-step-reframe technique
This is one of the most 'hypnotic' of all NLP techniques and as such the congruence, beliefs and state of the practitioner is key. You need to have the mind-set that your client absolutely does have the answer! Remember to genuinely thank the 'parts' involved' and remember to integrate fully at the end; we want our client to leave 'fully integrated.' With the client, you will work to:

1. Identify the pattern of behaviour to be changed (X)
2. Establish communication with the part that generates the behaviour. Go inside and ask the following question of yourself and be aware of how that part makes itself known to you. (what you can see, hear, feel etc). Perhaps as a symbol or image. Now ask that part, we'll call it part X, to confirm the signal for 'yes' and to do the opposite for 'no'.
3. Separate the intention from behaviour. Thank the part for responding. Now ask if it would be willing to let you know what its been trying to do for you by generating behaviour X. As you ask that question, once again be alert so you can detect the 'yes' or

'no' response. If you get a 'yes'; ask that part to reveal the positive intention. You can then move on to step 4. If you get a 'no' repeat step 3 to discover more.

4. Create alternative behaviour to satisfy the positive intention of that part. Now get the client to go inside, and contact the creative part of their personality and ask it to generate alternative behaviours that are just as good or better than behaviour X to satisfy the intention of the part we've been communicating with. Have the part responsible for X signal you with a 'yes' signal when it has at least three new behaviours.

5. Ask if part X would accept the new choices and the responsibility for generating them when needed. Now ask part X if it is willing to accept responsibility for generating new behaviours in appropriate contexts when its intention needs to be fulfilled, for the next four weeks.

6. Ecological check. Ask that part that has been responding to be unresponsive (still, silent, etc.) then ask if there are any parts that object to the negotiations that have just taken place and be alert to any internal response, (using all the modalities, visual auditory and kinaesthetic,) that occurs.

7. Now Go And Do It! - Test! Then Future Pace! Ensure full integration. *

Session 3: the origins of the habit
This session explores where the addictive behaviour started. I use regression techniques and explain them as an opportunity to: "look under the bed, and see what has created the scary shadows".

As much behaviour is unconscious, discovering the key events that have caused it will help the client put the pieces of the puzzle together for themselves. A sample session plan for this session might be:

- Review the changes of the past week and discuss as appropriate
- Review goals and actions taken towards them

- (Induce hypnosis)
- Timeline or Regression Techniques
- Positive Mental Rehearsal

Session 4: discovering how good the future can be
This session begins by reviewing the previous week's activity and discussing the changes and any other emotions that the previous session brought up.

The client and I review the goals sheet together and discuss the actions taken. This session would usually include a hypnosis session using a safe/relaxed place, a wise advisor or inner guide and a timeline to the future.

This allows the client to fully experience the richness that life has to offer, and can help bring about change and boost the client's mindset. Creating a positive expectancy is key to overcoming addictive habits as associating in (that is experiencing life through their own eyes) makes change possible and helps troubleshoot the decision-making process. For homework, the client will have a self-hypnosis or audio and will continue work on their goals sheet.

Session 5: finding the gaps
By finding gaps I mean, finding what's holding the client back? Confidence techniques at this stage can be key to promoting long-lasting lifestyle changes. Exploring the beliefs that are keeping the client from making those changes is vital. Where do these beliefs come from? Are they true? How would life be better if they adopted a better belief system? Do they believe that they will ever kick their addictive habits?

Confidence techniques are useful to boost your client's self-esteem and confidence levels. A technique that I like to kick start confidence work is the wipeclean technique.

Induce light hypnosis and ask your client to imagine either a blackboard, whiteboard or even a computer screen. This is no ordinary board as this is the board that they are going to project onto it, negative words, beliefs and sayings that either they themselves or other people have said to them. Once all the words are there, ask your client what they think about these negative words. The chances are, that when confronted with this, they can see how limiting these really are.

Now get your client to be really resourceful in removing these words, until finally the space is clear. Now that they have created a clean slate, you can ask them to project all of the really positive words about them, their qualities, strengths, achievements, and attributes. Maybe things that someone who really loves them would say?

Once this new board is complete, ask the client for their reflections of this new board. How will life be better now that they realise just how many resources they really have? Ask how this will improve their life going forward.

The client can then absorb this board, either by breathing those words in, or fixing it. A helpful exercise is to then imagine this map as part of the process that's going to help them forward in their future, a map or blueprint for their unconscious mind to follow,

I also use visualisation/aversion techniques, using hypnosis to take the client to their greatest fears. People generally avoid pain and seek pleasure so aversion therapy is really powerful here. Discovering your clients' greatest fear is powerful at creating behaviour change.

Common scenarios that I use include: visualising themselves becoming even fatter/bloated/ ill/ in hospital/ having heart attacks/ in the morgue/ seeing their own funeral/ their children being raised by another. These are powerful scenes that are often distressing to process. However, it is these new images that are likely to remain in the *'Library'* and be the ones that the *'PA'* references to see whether this addictive behaviour is helpful or not.

A positive mental rehearsal is useful for generating new

behaviour and allowing the client to experience this as well as including and rehearsing any challenges or blips that are likely to occur.

Session 6: keeping on the path
A review of the last two months takes place at this session, identifying the client's goals, new resources, connections, progress and actions that still need to be taken. This session looks at the long-term successes of the client and where any tweaks need to be made. A hypnosis session which works around the client's own beliefs, resources and plans for the future finishes the programme and the client learns how to use self-hypnosis to help themselves in the future.

This six-session programme is just a guide to get you started if you want to work in this area. Always, the client's individual needs should be your basis, rather than sticking to a strict pre-plan.

* Thanks to Richard Bandler and John Grinder.
www.nlptechniques.org

Want to know more?

You can find out more about Nicola at

www.axeingaddictions.co.uk where you can also

download her complimentary e-guide 7 Secrets to Overcoming Addiction. *At the website to go with this book (yourhypnotherapyniche.com) you can download case studies on dealing with alcohol addiction and cocaine addiction, a sample script for dealing with cocaine addiction and Nicola's diagram on how the brain works in the addiction cycle.*

Nicola is writing a book to help women overcome addictions in middle-age, this will be out next year. If you would like more information or to pre-order this book email annjaloba@btinternet.com

Chapter Five

Changing the mindset of the anxious executive

Claire McGrath, is Mrs Mindset. She is using her experience of the corporate world to help executives deal with their high stress environments. She describes the expertise needed to work with this lucrative client group

Anxiety is a naturally occurring state, designed to safeguard us from danger. However, feeling fearful in the *absence* of any danger shows something is wrong. It's usually when people start to feel out of control with their anxiety or fear that they seek help. Unfortunately, with corporate organisations, action is not usually taken until after the fire has started, when an executive is off work and is unable to function properly.

Where executives and directors are leading and managing from a state of anxiety, it is no surprise to find that their work life and mindset is negatively affected. Whether their anxiety is attributed to internal or external influences (or both), my aim is to get them to take responsibility for their reactions to these influences.

By challenging these reactions and re-labelling thinking patterns, we can start to create a domino effect, generating a positive outcome throughout the layers of the company.

Most of today's executives have huge pressures and

responsibilities. Here are some of the most common areas where you may be called upon to help executives with anxiety in their working life.

- Presentations. Feeling anxious prior to speaking to a group of people. This type of performance anxiety is also known as social anxiety
- Difficult people. The responsibility of having to deal with conflict or difficult people or situations can lead to inability to cope
- Where teams are not working together, redundancy notices, and conflict between employees. Increasingly, executives are being asked to manage their teams and are given more responsibility for the effectiveness of the team
- Perfectionism, where the executive places unrealistic expectations on themselves and their workload. This over-commitment is not only counter-productive, but can have serious psychological effects as the work/life balance suffers
- Change. Takeovers and mergers can be stressful for everyone in the organisation, not just executives and directors who are directly involved with the process. Restructuring of management or hierarchy, merging of departments, a change in who someone accounts for or reports to, a reduction in earnings or renewed status and even a change in title can all affect the comfort of familiar day-to-day routines. The problem we address here is not what will happen, but what the person fears will happen
- Travelling. The physiological effects of long haul flights, adjusting to different languages, changes in weather, different time zones and food can all take their toll
- Cultural differences. As well as managing racial or religious differences, new employees expectations also need to be met as they may be influenced by the culture of their previous organisation. A conversation I had with an executive demonstrates the conflict he felt about how different cultures

operate. The man in question was visiting a metal smelting factory in China where he noticed some employees were wearing flip flops and not meeting the health and safety standards customary in the UK. He raised his concerns only to be met with his Chinese counterpart's interpretation of the scene – if an accident happens, a workforce is so readily available these people can be easily replaced.

Physiological Symptoms
As more demands are put upon executives to achieve more in less time, pressure to perform increases, leading to a range of problems from headaches, depression, body rashes, indigestion, high blood pressure, ulcers and IBS. These are just a few of the physiological symptoms I have witnessed in my executive clientele over the years. In addition, stress can lead to some or all of the following:

o Poor sleep – inability to sleep, or waking during the night, disturbed by an ongoing internal dialogue. This lack of quality sleep leads to further tiredness and lethargy
o Difficulty making decisions – with so many thoughts going through the executive's head along with negative outcome predictions, it is no wonder they struggle to be decisive. They may then make poor choices, often losing valuable contracts or deadlines in the process
o Irritability and poor communication – feeling overwhelmed and an inability to cope with the pressures can lead to poor interactions and a feeling of hopelessness. Inadequate communication and ambiguity can lead to unnecessary conflicts and problems, misunderstandings and confusion
o Forgetfulness – overload can result in poor concentration and preoccupation with worries. A mindset of feeling like a fraud or not worthy of their role can ensue

This avalanche of negative thinking and experiences leads to the person failing to recognise and process the good things in life, failing to listen to their bodies, doing too much, and creating stress. Struggling with feeling anxious and finding situations a constant battle, they may resort to alcohol, drugs or gambling.

Companies increasingly understand and appreciate the psychological and economic costs of stress. Because of this more companies are prepared to invest in their employees' wellbeing. It makes good business sense to start with their top executives and business leaders.

The knowledge they gain about managing anxiety and maintaining a healthy mindset filters down through the company hierarchies.

Many companies make this a part of their company ethos. Organisations that incorporate, for example, mindfulness into the working day include Google, Twitter, Facebook, IBM and Unilever. Google managers practise a 2-minute meditation before meetings to increase effectiveness.

Working with the corporate world
If you want to approach the corporate world then firstly become really good at what you do. Create a page on your website detailing the workshops you can offer. Write some articles for Linked In. Write an article for a professional publication. Tell executives who you currently work with that you can offer workshops to their company.

For individual clients, there are two different types: those who have found you themselves and those whose company has contacted you. These need to be treated differently. In the first, the person will likely feel in control of their decision. A complimentary consultation can be undertaken by telephone at their initial enquiry. However in the second, where contact has been arranged through their company, the person often doesn't feel in control of the decision.

For this reason I conduct the initial information gathering at our first face-to-face meeting, rather than on the telephone.

However, I will want to speak to the employee by telephone prior to commencing therapy so I can manage their expectations. The HR department usually provide contact details so we can have a chat.

Initially, people can feel a little cautious and I always inform them of my confidentiality policy. Although their company may be funding their therapy, everything that is discussed remains confidential between us. I find that people naturally open up as the sessions progress and rapport develops. As the weeks pass, further disclosures and revelations unfold naturally. For example, when we work on beliefs in the first session, I ask them what they could do if they no longer had their symptoms, what they would like to change or achieve and why. This starts to get the imagination working in a more positive way.

The number of sessions can range from five to 12, depending on the issues involved. Initially, I like to see people on a weekly basis. As therapy progresses the time between sessions can lengthen.

Formulating a treatment plan: the background
Be mindful of how a typical executive thinks. Their mindset is usually one of thinking that they should be perfect and should be able to cope (notice the use of the word 'should'). Presenting themselves for help can often be seen as a sign of failure.
Aim to encourage your client to:

- Suspend judgement and self-criticism and avoid anticipatory anxiety
- Respond to events in a calm manner to benefit their heart, head and body
- Recognise, slow down and step away from negative reactions to everyday events
- Respond more effectively to difficult or challenging situations
- Achieve balance and resilience at work and at home

○ Be fully present in their life and work so they can improve their quality of life. Throughout your sessions work on cultivating realistic expectations and goals so the client is capable of following them through and achieving success. Encourage positive self-esteem, help the client to acquire confidence in abilities including recognising strengths, and developing problem-solving skills and skills in managing feelings.

A treatment plan: what you need to do
Anxiety assessment
Firstly, we want to establish how anxiety is affecting the individual. There are many anxiety-measuring tools which enable the therapist to assess and measure the severity of a client's anxiety. These can be useful in determining the extent of the anxiety; mild, moderate or severe. A commonly used tool is the Generalised Anxiety Disorder Questionnaire (GAD-7).

These tools help to make the process measurable and give the client a sense of ownership and an insight into the extent that their anxiety is affecting them. From here, their individual treatment plan is formulated. This includes the style of therapy that is best suited to them and an insight into how we are going to create change.

Coué's Law
Take some time to explain Coué's Law (also known as the law of reversed effort) and be prepared for questions.

You may know this concept, but just because the person sitting in front of you is a chief executive doesn't mean he or she does.

Emile Coué was a French psychologist and pharmacist who introduced a psychological technique based on positive suggestion and autosuggestion. Coue's Law states that when the conscious mind is in conflict with the unconscious (or imagination) then the imagination will always win. An example would be someone telling themselves 'Don't get anxious'. The person's imagination is now focused on getting anxious. The resultant emotions accompany this imagined scenario of 'not feeling anxious'. Hey presto, the person feels anxious by the mere act of telling themselves not to! So if your client wants to achieve a goal and the imagination is focused on what could go wrong, they will create the feelings and emotions which focus on the opposite of what they actually want to achieve. Coue's Law demonstrates the importance of focusing on what you want, not on what you don't want.

After this, it will then make sense to your client to take some time out to use their imagination and reflect on their goals. Get them to rehearse how they want to see themselves and then to make a commitment to focus their mind for a few minutes every day to cultivate a positive mindset. Focusing the mind can help to eliminate debilitating symptoms such as anxiety and panic attacks within a matter of weeks. Doing this daily will help change the direction of the client's life.

Chevreul's Pendulum
It is worth conducting this valuable demonstration which explains the ideomotor response (IMR). The IMR shows how the body can experience a physical reaction without the person being aware of the movement.

Michel-Eugene Chevreul, a French chemist demonstrated the earliest explanation of the IMR. He spent time researching the popular parlour games of the time such as dowsing rods, magic pendulums and table turning. In his 1854 paper he explains how muscular reactions, although involuntary and unconscious, produce movements which can appear magical.

Known as Chevreul's Pendulum, this demonstration reveals how, by focusing on a thought the client can actually cause a bodily reaction. Just as the body reacts to pain, the body can also react with a negative IMR to ideas, words or images such as 'Business Flight' or 'Conference'. This demonstration of the power our thoughts have over our mind and body shows how powerful our thoughts are and gives the individual the responsibility to change those negative thoughts. It shows the remarkable effects of auto-suggestion in action and how the body reacts physically to imagined scenes. (Wikipedia 2015)

It also goes some way to explain conversion hysteria. Also known as conversion disorder or functional neurological symptom disorder, this is a condition whereby people convert psychological stress into physical symptoms. Typical symptoms include numbness, blindness, paralysis, rashes and impaired speech or co-ordination. Symptoms can arise in response to perceived stressful events. It is important to be able to explain this concept to your client as they will realise there is nothing wrong with them, they were simply focusing on the wrong thing.

Useful Models
The GROW (Goal, Reality, Options, What) model is very useful when used with effective open questions. This model helps to create a sense of responsibility and motivation and not allow past experiences to limit future goals.

Much used in business training, the competence learning cycle has 4 stages – unconscious incompetence, conscious incompetence, conscious competence and unconscious competence. The cycle takes the executive from low performance to recognition of their weak areas, to using effort to improve and finally to spontaneous, natural high performance.

The Myers Briggs Type Indicator (MBTI) which is based on 4 approaches helps the executive to gain self insight and an awareness of how conflict may arise with colleagues who have a different style of thinking.

Beliefs
I want to know my client's beliefs about themselves: how powerful they feel in relation to their work, as well as their beliefs about their ability to change their anxiety. This tells me a lot about their locus

of control. First thing is to listen to their concerns. Every executive, depending on their role, will have different concerns and needs. Then we work on their self-belief.

Recognising that they are a human being with human emotions that are perfectly normal is often a huge relief. Just because they occupy a high-ranking position doesn't mean they are immune to emotions.

It's okay to feel frightened, out of your depth, or worried that you will lose control. An explanation of how our thoughts affect our beliefs about our abilities, our place in the world and how we perceive how others perceive us is useful to add in at this point. I talk about whether that person has become a human *doing* rather than a human *being*!

Emotional Intelligence
Psychologist Daniel Goleman highlighted the value of emotional intelligence (EQ) over academic or mental ability (IQ).

His research demonstrated that, for good working relationships, EQ was twice as important than IQ for workplace effectiveness and success. Put simply, emotional intelligence is about developing social skills such as self awareness and awareness of others. The resulting improved relationships make the executive's life easier and gives them a valuable tool to manage themselves and others.

Awareness
An aspect of mindset work is the client being aware of when they're not being positive.

We look at methods of looking for the silver lining in just about everything – from the coffee provided at meetings to the practical use of time whilst sitting in a traffic jam! We examine the choices available to get off the negative roundabout and start focusing on the positive side of events – the choice of having a positive or a negative mindset and ways to use their choice to achieve a positive outlook. By developing an optimistic attitude they are able effectively to balance negative emotions with positive ones.

Time management
Most executives are aware of time management yet do little to implement this in their lives. Much of their valuable time is wasted in time-sapping meetings or wading through insignificant emails.

We examine using time well including who or what they allow to share their time and creating time for fun and family. This includes using energy well – letting go of any grievances and disagreements and freeing up mental energy by letting go of grudges. Spending time relaxing or enjoying self hypnosis. In the words of Sydney J Harris: "The time to relax is when you don't have time for it". Taking time out can give valuable head space to revisit problems with clarity.

Distress tolerance and resilience
This is another area worth examining.

Distress tolerance addresses how to tolerate pain in difficult situations, for example where it is outside of the client's control so they cannot change it. So tolerate the boring lunch meeting or the boring boss – you'll be home in an hour; tolerate the irritating junior who keeps interrupting – they'll soon know the ropes.

Tolerate any feelings of distress, it's not the end of the world and the roof is not going to cave in. Resilience describes a person's ability to adapt to perceived stressful situations and adversity. Executive stress can come in the form of workplace concerns such as financial crises, redundancy or new working environments. We work on acquiring resilience by developing individual coping strategies.

This allows the client to work effectively through any risk factors. This could be changing the thought process, removing themselves from the situation, getting perspective and creating an internal locus of control.

External and Internal control orientation
This is a vital area to address when working with executives as their beliefs will affect job satisfaction, stress levels and how successful they will be within their organisation. Their beliefs about their ability to affect outcomes and events in their life will determine their current locus of control (locus is Latin for place). When you have sufficiently explained locus of control they will see how anxiety and related symptoms can be remedied in quite a short space of time. People with high internal locus of control (internal control orientation) believe that they will receive reinforcement based upon their own actions. By contrast, people with high external locus of control (external control orientation) believe that regardless of their own actions, their fate rests in the hands of luck, fate, or other, more powerful entities, perhaps their boss!

We look at how nothing is set in stone. If that was the case the client wouldn't be able to learn a new skill or how to use a new piece of software. They are not 'an anxious person' as that would suggest it is a set or fixed disorder. We work to show it is only their belief about a situation and this can be changed.

If the client believes that outcomes are outside of their personal control (external control orientation) then they are unlikely to take steps to change how they think about it. I was talking to a group of business executives recently whose workplace had caught fire. With an internal locus, they could see that it isn't the fire that is affecting them (although they did have to relocate) but rather how they perceived it.

If they believe that the outcomes of their actions are dependent on what they do (putting it into perspective, recognising no one was killed etc.) as opposed to the events being outside of their control (we're helpless, life is scary, I've lost all my work, what's the point etc.) they will manage the situation more effectively. It is the same situation. There were different opinions about the fire (some worrying constantly about it happening again versus those who were just getting on with settling into their new surroundings). This showed it cannot be the actual fire that is affecting them. Their locus says a lot about how they will deal with the effects of the fire and the relocation.

Conducting a locus of control test is an invaluable resource for helping your client to challenge themselves on some of their limiting beliefs and develop a more internal locus.

There are many loci of control tests widely available on the Internet. The original questionnaire was developed by Julian Rotter (1966). Many others such as Terry Pettijohn (author of Psychology: A ConnecText) have refined and developed their own tests based on Rotter's.

Find one that suits you or develop your own to fit in with your niche. Whichever you use, remember there are no right or wrong answers – it is a quiz which describes the degree to which the person believes that outcomes result from their behaviour or whether they come from forces outside their control. A low score indicates an internal locus and a high score an external locus.

Brooding
Overthinking or brooding is a useful trait when the person has an internal locus of control. Brooding with an external locus however can lead to overthinking things outside of their control and dwelling over negative events. Let the client recognise:

- That they are not the emotion; they generate the emotion because of how they perceive or process the situation
- Signs of brooding such as living in the past, worrying about the future and comparing past experiences and using this to negatively predict future events
- How brooding can lead to a constant stream of worry and not being present in or enjoying the present moment. "My life has been a series of tragedies – none of which actually happened" as Mark Twain said

Gratitude exercise
This exercise is all about recognising the good things that they actually achieve. Get the client to write down 7 positive things that have happened during the past month. Then explore how they have instigated each of those 7 events and recognise how they have been responsible for them happening. For example, my boss said I'd done a good job – that's because I put extra time into writing that report.

The gratitude exercise is used 3 times or more per day, first thing in the morning (looking at the list will set them up for a happy successful day), middle of the day and last thing at night. Busy people tend to forget or overlook achievements as they start focusing on the next goal. The gratitude exercise helps them to develop awareness and process the positive things they have achieved. It also helps to think upon waking that: 'yes I'm alive and the whole day is up to me.'

Interpersonal effectiveness
Most executives like the feeling of being in control and therefore learning to say no can be very difficult.

Explore the possibilities of asking for what the client wants (for example reducing to a four-day week) and saying no (for example, the project is too much to take on at the moment) whilst maintaining self-respect and good working relationships. Clients often take on too much because of a fear of what people might think of them (social anxiety) and a desire to appear in control, strong and able. Taking time to think about the consequence of agreeing to every request is a sign of good management and not a sign of weakness. Being afraid to say no can also indicate over-compensating for a lack of confidence.

Self Esteem
Your client's self worth and self evaluation will likely be at an all time low. How they see themselves (not coping, letting their

company and family down) will play a huge part in how they feel about themselves. This will underpin everything they say and do, how they act and interact. Introduce a self-esteem exercise and explain its positive benefits. Here is an example
1. Recognise that inner voice and say 'Stop' when aware of negative thoughts
2. Write down 5 things that they appreciate about their life
3. Stop trying to be perfect, recognise when they are comparing
4. Process the positive things in life and play down any negatives
5. Spend some time doing something they enjoy
6. Spend time with people who energise and value them
7. Recognise the benefits of a high self-esteem

Perspective and perfectionism
Often my clients take themselves and life too seriously.

I will always challenge them on perspective. I will say: "Just because the report is late are you going to lose your job? We want to look at evidence to the contrary, for example let's look at how many times you have submitted your work on time." Suffering from anxiety doesn't mean they are a failure. Many famous people suffer with feeling anxious – Barbara Streisand, Adele, Whoopi Goldberg and Johnny Depp to name just a few. Get your client to write down their strengths and in so doing they can become aware of any weaknesses and accept that we can't all be 100 per cent perfect at everything 100 per cent of the time. However they can work on their weaknesses. Accept that sometimes we may need help and that's okay too.

Failure
People who never fail are those who play it safe and don't take risks. Those people rarely achieve. We look at how it's okay to abandon a project which is doomed, or change your mind. We look at how every failure can be turned into a valuable lesson in how not to do something. A fragile executive ego may find it difficult

to accept or consider the possibility of failure and consequently will never learn from mistakes. Encourage clients to do the self-esteem exercise so they have the coping skills. Look at how risk and failure go hand in hand, as does risk and success.

Lighten up
Laugh at yourself, and don't take yourself so seriously. I do a wonderful visualisation which is very useful when the client feels out of their depth or anxious about a forthcoming event. This exercise is also very useful for helping with perfectionism and gaining perspective on a problem.

I get the client to close their eyes, take three deep breaths and imagine that they are as light and free as the air around them.

Then I say: "Now imagine that you are floating upwards higher and higher, leaving behind all the problems, feeling them dropping from you as you simply float higher and higher. Now imagine that you are freely floating in space, with nothing but the lovely velvety warm darkness of space all around you.

Surrounded by a lovely warm darkness and nothing but space in any direction.

Now imagine looking down at the earth, as beautiful as it is, you know it isn't a perfect place. Now imagine floating down gently as gentle as a tiny feather until you are over Europe, as beautiful as it looks from up high you know that it isn't a perfect place.

Continue floating down and down until you are over (England/Scotland/whatever country they live in). Now continue to float down and down until you are over (Gloucestershire/Yorkshire whatever county they live in).

Now floating down into this room keeping that warm relaxation with you. Bring your awareness back to the room, aware of the chair beneath you, the sound of my voice. Take 3 deep breaths and on the third outward breath open your eyes back to now and back to this room."

We then look at how beautiful the world, this country, county and town may be, but how none of it is 100 percent perfect. So why try so hard to be perfect in a world that isn't perfect anyway? This gives perspective on the upcoming annual assessment, yearly accounts or new project.

I hope you have found this run-through working with executives useful. It can be demanding, it can be stimulating and very lucrative and you can really know when you are making a difference, which is what I love about it.

References
Wikipedia 2105https://en.wikipedia.org/wiki/Ideomotor_phenomenon

Want to know more?

You can find out more about Claire's corporate programmes for stressed executives at www.mrsmindset.co.uk Read Mrs Mindset's case studies including how she helped someone who was gambling heavily, and someone who had been on long term sick leave at yourhypnotherapyniche.com

Chapter Six

Developing a specialist niche in coaching

Ann Jaloba has developed a successful business, coaching and publishing books to help therapists develop their businesses. She describes why hypnotherapists make the best coaches and how to specialise as a coach

I believe that no-one is better at coaching than a well-trained and focused hypnotherapist. If you are an experienced hypnotherapist you already have a shed load of tools and skills which are invaluable if you decide to move over to the closely-related niche of coaching. If you are an expert in another professional field that is even better, because you can carve out a specialist coaching niche.

This is a pretty controversial view. To read much of the literature out there you would think that coaching and therapy have nothing in common and you will even come across arguments that they should be kept apart at all costs.

Partly, this comes from a complete misunderstanding of what therapy is. To take one example among many, Anthony M. Grant, the founder and director of the Coaching Psychology Unit at the University of Sydney in Australia talks about the common belief that therapy deals with the past and coaching deals with the future. Any decent hypnotherapist will know that, although we may address events and beliefs in the past which have held our client back, to move a client on from their current problem involves focusing on their future. We are all about the future and helping clients have a *better* future and these are the skills you can take into coaching. If you have any experience of supervising colleagues then you are even better placed as you will have much practise of using techniques such as solution-focused questioning to help people make the right life choices and career choices to enhance their professional life.

There are as many different definitions of coaching as there are coaches. For clarity, I am using the term to mean a set-up where a coach and a customer (or coachee) agree to work together to develop new ways of doing or find solutions to a particular issue or set of issues. This process can involve looking at life choices in a very broad way to working out how to achieve a detailed and narrow life or business aim.

Because this definition is so broad coaching can sometimes seem overly vague and woolly. I am sure many of you have had the experience of listening to coaches, perhaps in an online session, and coming away to realise that you have not learned anything new. This is why I suggest developing a specialist niche within coaching. You can then be sure you are offering something concrete and of value and this will make sure you are standing out from the rest.

If you want to move into this field, I would recommend that you hone and develop your skills as a therapist. A useful way of doing this is to undertake some training in the field of supervision. This can give you an in-depth training in skills including: how to work with someone to use their knowledge to solve the issues which they bring to you; building rapport; working with the customer's modalities, values and beliefs; and using solution-focused questioning.

If you decide to do a coaching course, I would recommend you do the following: all these courses offer free tasters so pick the

niche coaching

one which looks like it suits you best and then do this test. If the speaker doesn't tell you something which you don't know in 10 minutes then avoid them and look for another course.

I have mentioned specialising or nicheing, and if you want to move into coaching I would advise that you specialise or niche in an area where you have an expertise and professional knowledge as well as your therapy skills. If you are wondering if you can to do this then see if you can answer three questions.

1) What group do you want to work with?
2) What can you offer which isn't out there already?
3) What you can do better than that which is currently on offer?

If you are still not sure, do this thought experiment. Imagine you are talking to your target audience for an hour. How many things can you tell them which you can be reasonably sure they do not already know? If you have a niche, a specialism where you are a real expert, you will be able to tell them a lot.

So, for me I can tell people how to write a book or a press release or an article for a magazine or a blog post or copy for their website. I can do this because I have spent over 30 years as a journalist and I call on those skills and that knowledge. And I can talk about it until the cows come home, I know it inside out. That is my niche and people who pay me because they want something in this area are getting value for money.

But if I was speaking to an audience of, say, amateur runners about how to improve sports performance I would be filling in the time with generalities and platitudes which I would bet my audience knew already. And they would realise this pretty quickly and go somewhere else.

This approach goes against the orthodoxy which says coaching should be content-free and coaching and training are separate. Well, they are not really, if you are coaching well and moving your customer to some real changes then pretty soon you will hit the barrier of your expertise and knowledge of the area where they want to develop. There *is* a content-free bit to coaching – it is at the beginning where you determine what the customer needs and wants.

After that, if you are serious about helping your customer achieve, you are going to need to give much more specialist advice (and even training if your customer is missing a skill which they need). It might be that you provide this or you might refer the customer to another expert, you will know which to do if you keep your customer's goal in mind.

Specialisation in coaching seems to me to be common sense. Why would you want to see a coach who understands nothing about what you want to achieve and would not know how to get you there?

But if you do have expert skills in a professional field and want to go into this coaching, then you can marry those with your therapy skills and you have a great future ahead.

For me, moving into coaching people to write books (and then moving into publishing from there) was something which arose from the therapy work I was doing. It felt right and was relatively easy. An increasing amount of my work is now in helping people get their ideas into print and publishing books. It is this specialist niche which is growing fastest for me.

Where to start with your customer
So what exactly do I do when someone walks through my door?

I use all my therapy skills first; it feels natural to move from showing clients how to reach *their* potential to showing my coaching customers how to do the same.

My work as a therapist has always been goal-directed; I like to think people come to me to solve an issue or set of issues as part of their life journey, not *to replace* their life journey. In my world, the client and I work together, we explore the issues and come up with a plan, and we carry on working together to get this absolutely right, testing it out along the way. The client then goes away equipped to live what they feel is a successful and fulfilled life. So clients who come to me want to be more fulfilled in their lives, whether they want a big change or a little tweak to put them into a better place. This always involves the client deciding what to do and then receiving my professional help in how to do it. This model translates very well into coaching.

If you move into coaching most customers will come to you with one of two mindsets. The first have a sense that they are stuck and cannot move on, they are not sure where to go next to fulfil themselves in both their work and their life. The second have a clearer idea of where they want to go, but lack the confidence or knowledge of how to get there.

So initially, you will be finding out what the customer's vision is and what is holding them back from achieving this. You will be working with them on their belief system and world view and you will be helping them to focus on their abilities and build their self-esteem.

To do this well, you will be relying on your very solid therapy skills. So, using solution-focused questioning, you can help them towards their next steps, and then you can use future pacing and visualisation techniques to help them explore possible options. Sometimes you can use hypnotherapy to help build self-esteem. Anchoring and breathing techniques to control nerves will also be useful tools. Goal setting and tasking are absolutely essential as you help your customer begin to make the practical steps to achieve what they want. So far, so good. And at this point I bring in the idea of specialisation, and here I believe you need to be an expert in a particular field.

The point where a specialist coach is needed
I will help anyone find their direction, but once the customer has decided on what that is, I will *only* continue to work with them if they want to develop in an area where I have *real* expertise.

For me, this is usually in my main niche of writing for

publication (books, press releases, magazine articles, blogs, whatever fits the customer's needs and goals) – often my customers can do one and want to branch out, or they write a lot in their business and know that a whole book is the next step. I will also keep working with people who want to become hypnotherapists or develop NLP skills to use in their work and I will work with people in certain professional fields (ones which I know well) who want to progress.

I made this decision, because I believe strongly that you need this personal experience, knowledge and skills to do anything useful. So here is my rule. Once my coaching customer has decided on their direction, I will continue to work with them only if I have more skills and knowledge than they do in the area in which they want to develop.

Some coaches would disagree, but I believe this is the main reason why coaching sometimes gets a bad press. Nearly everyone reading this book will have had the experience of spending money for a one-to-one session or joining a group, which promises to help you make your business a success for example, to be told what we know already. Or as a colleague of mine puts it: "The cult of the bleeding obvious."

So here is an example of a potential customer who it would be hard for me to help. If a customer came to me saying that they wanted to get on to the board of a new technology company, but lacked the confidence to get there, I will ask how can I help? Or to be more exact, how *far* can I help. Certainly, I can use many of my skills to do some general confidence boosting, I may be able, by the use of regression techniques, to overcome and address some issues which are holding that person back. But eventually, because I know nothing about new technology companies, I know I am likely to run into a brick wall.

So right from the beginning I would be looking for someone who has that expertise to whom I can refer that customer at the appropriate time.

Using other experts

Even when you are working within your comfort zone, don't dismiss how useful it can be to recommend at least one session with a different sort of expert.

This is a story from someone I have consulted as a customer and greatly admire. She is Jane Chapman (from True Colours Image Consultancy in South Yorkshire), a brilliant style consultant. She told me about a client she had who was looking to expand her work from the corporate financial sector to the charity world. The client was noticing that people at networking events were not greeting her with open arms, to put it mildly. The client, as an experienced networker, was nonplussed by this and didn't know what she was doing wrong. Jane was able to identify the issue, the client's clothes were too formal and sending the wrong message, a few changes, a less structured jacket and different colours, worked miracles At the next meeting she was not only warmly welcomed, but booked three follow-on meetings.

I couldn't have done that! But now I know where to send my coaching customers who need an image change to fit with what they do.

And there is another lesson there, the importance of building a network of expert professionals. So network, be honest about what you don't know and have a book of contacts full of people who do know. Refer clients on if you honestly think someone else knows more about that area and how to help that client.

How I structure my sessions

I am perfectly happy to see customers who have the vague feeling that they are not fulfilling themselves in life and will happily accept those who tell me they want a 'life coach'.

Typically, these customers will fall into two categories. The first is someone who wants something but is not sure what it is, the second is someone who knows what they want but has blocks to getting it. In such cases, I know my skills, as a hypnotherapist and a supervisor can help most of these people to more clarity.

I usually recommend four sessions to get a coaching customer to a place where they can move forward.

Session One: relax and focus techniques
I begin by helping convince the person in front of me that they can change. Often they will be stuck and anxious so I show, by simple stress relieving techniques that they can help themselves feel better. Then I introduce the idea of the 'habits of positive thinking'. I talk to them about the evidence of what really makes people happy. I move on to questioning my customer about what will make them happy. This may not even be in the same ball park as what they have been chasing. Skilled questioning and visioning can move the most confusing of scenarios to the conclusion which is right for them.

Calm and focus and making the space to think about these matters are important here, so I often teach self hypnosis in this session and ask the customer to use it to take the time to explore the different options we have looked at.

Session Two: focus on what is achievable
This session is hard-talking, realistic and wonderful. The customer will have more of an idea what they want now and most of the work is about how to get there. Often the key thing here is to find out what is holding them back.

I spend a lot of time helping the client explore if what they want is achievable and possible.

Much sub-NLP nonsense is talked about how it is possible to achieve anything you want. It isn't. A 50-year-old is not going to become a professional footballer; a 5'2" girl will not make it as a top fashion model. At this point I use questioning skills to draw out what it is about the ambition the customer has which is really driving them, what really matters to them.

My aim is to take the core of that dream and fulfil it by directing a set of actions to something realistic, but wonderful. To do this, I work in a solution-focused way. Take the prospective fashion model: I would find out what exactly that girl sees when she imagines she is on the catwalk (I will use hypnosis here because often this vision is stronger and clearer in hypnotic trance) and what feelings is she having that are most valuable to her. Does she want admiration and the enjoyment which comes from being in the public eye? Then perhaps working in a field where she is 'on show' such as events management will work? Or perhaps it is about the clothes? Then a career in fashion or styling may beckon? Over time, we move towards a possible reality which is fulfilling for her.

In this session, it is quite common for customers to realise that what they think they wanted is not what they really want. Some people think they want what everyone around them has always told them they want and their key to happiness and development is to find that this is not true.

So I refer back as well as forward, asking when the customer felt happiest. If they felt happiest as a shop assistant when they were 22 then perhaps the desire to become a surgeon was misplaced? Or perhaps not. That is what the challenge and the delight of the process is – finding out the unexpected.

Session Three: goals and getting there
In this session I try to be more specific, but do this while recognising that specifics need good soil, so I help the customer build confidence in their own abilities and desires.

Sometimes I will find blocks and I am not afraid to use all my skills, including therapy skills to help.

There are two common examples. People at this stage often demonstrate certain mind traits that are not very helpful. 'grasshopper mind', jumping about from one idea to another and wild swings in confidence, are very common.

Negative thoughts and 'stopping' self-talk can also appear. That voice which is telling the customer 'I can't' can sometimes take direct therapeutic work to shift. I try to be flexible and transparent and not make false distinctions between coaching and therapy. If the customer is stuck then I have no hesitation in using therapy skills to help them unblock. (Remember that coaches who dismiss this approach are often those who do not have the skills to do it. As therapists, we have those skills and therefore an advantage in this field).

I encourage the customer to set achievable and measurable goals for one month, six months and one year (at least). To help them do this, I work backwards, starting with the final goal and then working out the steps necessary to get there. This is a very motivational way of working as it keeps the big goal clear in the mind, while the immediate and achievable steps can be celebrated daily.

At this point knowing my limits as a coach can be important. As we develop goals if I find I do not understand enough about the area then I refer the customer to an expert in that field.

Session Four: reflection and development
At this point the customer should have a fair idea about what they want to change and how they are going to do this and they will have made some steps to start.

I ensure that the customer has a clear picture of what they are achieving week-by-week, encouraging them to keep a diary or record and reminding them of how they were when they first came to see me.

I will often be working in my niche area by this point, so if we are working towards writing for publication, for example, we will have worked out a timetable which starts with a publication date and works backwards from there.

The customer will have certain tasks to carry out and if they get stuck I will look at what the issue is: confidence, focus, or lack of skill are all common blocks and I do whatever is necessary to work to overcome these. Often training can be necessary here to help the customer go forward. With my publishing or writing customers I can offer this, if the need is out of my area I will refer on.

Coaching in a specialist area
I find this truly satisfying and also very successful. It is much easier to stand out from the crowd; there will not be many others who have that mix of professional expertise and therapy skills which you are offering if you move into specialist coaching.

In my 'writing a book for business' niche, my coaching begins by finding out why the customer wants to write a book. This is important as it determines the look and feel of the finished product.

Then we choose a title and cover image, again this pins down exactly what they book is about – a book without a strong message will not do its job. Then I help the client to get going – I offer them a way of organising their information and help them divide that information into logical chapters. Then we move onto gathering information and the actual writing. This is followed by advice on checking for quality and how to publish. Finally, we discuss a marketing plan.

How this works is different for each customer. Some need more help to get their idea clear before they start. Others need some practical advice on how to write, or help with research, or guidance on how to divide the book into chapters

Here coaching goes alongside practical progress in writing and, if I am doing my job well, the customer is producing good quality writing which is targeted at their particular aim. Working together, we can be sure that they will soon have something which will help them build a more successful business. Progress is made at every session and the customer can see that progress.

I truly feel that I am giving value for money by using so many different skills and a lifetime of professional knowledge. I would have paid a coach to have got me there more quickly than I did!

Want to know more?

Ann coaches people who want to write to build their business through her Your Book for Business programme. She has recently moved into publishing and will be helping many of the contributors to this book bring out a book of their own. If you would like Ann's help contact her at www.yourbookforbusiness.com

You can get more advice on writing by visiting yourhypnotherapyniche.com

Chapter Seven

From fear of flying to flying fabulously

Philip Ayers loves to fly. Microlights, stunt flights and light aircraft are all fun to him. He uses this knowledge and joy to change the way his clients feel. Here, he describes the techniques he uses to get people flying

If we were meant to fly, then God would have given us wings. Well he did in the shape of aeroplanes! And now more than 8 million people fly every single day. This adds up to over 3 billion passengers a year, and this is still rising.

Yet many of us fear flying (Aviophobia). According to some estimates, as many as 25 percent of all Americans suffer some nervousness about flying and it can affect the person's whole life. However, a fear of flying or a full-blown phobia, (a phobia is a more out-of-control fear) are both treatable.

Fortunately, I love to fly and have flown light aircrafts and microlights as well as being in simulator and stunt flights. I feel comfortable in helping my clients over their fear of flying.

If you want to work with fear of flying, it is important to have a good knowledge of how flying works. So make sure you understand, aviation, weather, what causes turbulence and the like.

You're not trying to get your PPL (Private Pilots License) but rather gathering a little more information that will assist the fear of flying client to conquer their fear. You can source information at the library, on the Internet or better still get yourself to a local flying club to see what's on offer as these guys are the specialists and will guide and support you. It can also be good fun for the whole family!

Finding the problem and avoidance
One good place to start is finding the real cause of the client's problem. This is a *big* answer to getting clients over their fear.

Let me explain, I had a client who came to see me about his flying fear and how bad he felt.

On deeper questioning, we found out that it was the drive to the airport that was the instigator. This is what had happened. When he was much younger, he was in a car accident on the way to an airport. His unconscious had made the wrong connections by associating this with the fear of flying. This was one of those moments when he realised that his flying fear wasn't a fear of flying at all. Once we clarified this through therapy, his fear dissipated.

Questioning a client can unearth the real problem, as opposed to what the client may *think* is their problem. Here is another example.

A client who feared flying, was soon in a light aircraft flying and piloting the plane himself with the instructor at his side. Nevertheless going on larger aircraft was a bigger deal. We found that his over-anxiousness, was not a fear of flying, but walking through the tunnels to board the plane.

This phenomenon of people misdiagnosing themselves as having a fear of flying can be fascinating as you uncover it and help the client come to a new revelation about themselves. The fear may be a fear of leaving family behind, being burgled, or travelling on a busy motorway. Some clients are claustrophobic on the plane (fear of enclosed space), or fearful of heights. Some will have fear triggered by hearing or witnessing bad news of air crashes or disasters.

Then there is fear of not being in control, concerns about understanding a foreign language at the destination, or worry about what the destination is going to be like. Other clients may become over-anxious about flight delays or lost luggage. Of course last but not least the client may just be frightened to fly! It is important to notice the many variables which can present as a fear of flying.

Often the potential client will have had this fear for many years, yet they have never sought help. Sometimes, the avoidance has worked great in the past, but just because the client has avoided flying up until now, doesn't mean to say that they will never be put in a position where they *need* to fly. Some common examples where avoidance is no longer possible are: a new relationship with a partner who likes to travel by plane; a need to visit a close family member as this could be the last time you see them; taking a child to Disney Land; the big promotion which means taking business trips abroad.

Also, a fear of flying can impact on the client's whole family, restricting what they do. Family members, who don't share the client's fear, will not experience how the client really feels, and how stressful it can be and this can cause tension.

So avoidance is only a very limited solution, it is much better to remedy the fear.

How can hypnotherapy or related therapies help?
Often a client will tell you they have a fear of flying, they know how safe flying is, but this doesn't compute in their brain and their fear still persists. They realise how irrational this thought is, but they cannot cure this.

Meta questioning is the key to determining the client's real fear. This will quickly find out if it is the fear of flying or something related. This form of questioning can reach down to the client's deeper problems, when a client comes to realise what their real issue is.

Once both you and the client have a greater understanding of the answer, as the therapist, you even question that answer until you chunk it down to the basic foundations of their problem.

So a client may say: "I don't like planes" the question can be: "what is it about planes you don't like?" They might say they get claustrophobic (fear of enclosed spaces), you question this as a new lead and ask when was the first time they recognised this problem? And so you dig ever deeper.

Reframing the client's thinking is important at the start. For example, when working with fear of flying, you may find out that the client heard about a plane crash from the news. Then a re-frame of the media can help. Any good therapist will understand how the mass media works, how it instills fear into a vulnerable waiting public. I say to my clients that their TV is the hypnotist in their living room. So with any re-frame it is about how you change beliefs, attitudes, or ideas towards these events.

A client may come to you who was okay about flying, but has heard about a plane crash and now feels they cannot fly. You could reframe this by saying: "You've heard about a plane crash? . . . How would you feel if you hadn't heard about the crash? . . . Or are you surprised that planes crash? . . . Or after this accident, I hear that they are giving all the planes a good safety inspection which can only be a good thing, can it not?"

I find that Transactional Analysis (TA) therapy can also be useful here. Within the body and mind, we as people will react accordingly to what mode we are in. We have a playful child within us all just as we have an adult, a grown-up who acts sensibly, also we have the parent within us and this part in us will parent anyone or anything and is all about taking care. Of course the parent and child within us can be split, so, for example, you can have a nurturing parent or a critical one.

Once you determine the mode which your client is running, you can start to inform them of how this part has infiltrated the other parts of their personality. So if a person is in total 'critical parent mode', then this will affect the adult and child part of them.

By bringing this to their attention you can help them change. Most fears are generated when the client is in child mode even though they are an adult, so do your work on this. (The PAC Parent, Adult and Child). This is where we all respond from when we react to a stimulus causing a fear of flying. Once you explain this to a client, you can see their minds processing this new information.

This then leads to a greater awareness of their situation and starts to dissolve their problem naturally.

I like to think of this as removing all the client's obstacles before I put them into their trance.

They are probably already running themselves in a negative state of fear. This is a trance that *they* have unknowingly put themselves into and it is your job to take them out of that negative, fearful, illusion trance. By getting them to be relaxed and confident you can place them into a positive trance. This becomes their default way of thinking. Once out of a child/victim state their mind will recover much quicker.

Eye Movement Desensitization Reprocessing
E.M.D.R. (Eye Movement Desensitization Reprocessing) is a very useful therapy for fear of flying.

This therapy shows the client how to move their eyes in a way that gets them to process their problem; allowing it to give them internal clarity. This helps them resolve what they thought was their big fear. I find that this therapy can help when a client cannot come to terms with the irrationality of their behaviour.

To help my clients understand, I use this analogy. I say that EMDR will help unblock their barrier to their unconscious mind, so the two halves of the brain can talk to each other again. This helps their mind to make sense of the problem, so in this case it stops the fear being in control by putting them back in the driving seat. I tell them that their unconscious mind is like a washing machine, it will wash off all the negative thinking they have added to their fear.

When using EMDR you also get the chance to put some positivity into the client's thinking. The likelihood is that you instill confidence to fly, by bringing up the client's internal level to actually wanting this. Using the technique of EMDR helps the client to be more positive on a cognitive conscious level.

Of course there are many more techniques that you can use to help, but you have to see how well a client is responding to any therapy that you offer to know its effectiveness. Keeping a journal on how or what is more effective will greatly enhance your success rate with a client as they all respond differently.

Last, but not least, is the use of hypnotherapy. I believe that telling your client what to expect can increase the trance experience and let the client leave you at the end of their session with a positive outcome.

Even though I can get a result without always having to use hypnosis, I find that the client can feel cheated if you don't give them the opportunity to experience a trance. So whatever happens I always do the trance as this locks it all into place after the previous work that I've done.

So you have already re-framed the client's negative thinking and you've got them into a relaxed state. Then explain how the relaxing trance will work by telling them what they will get out of this experience (to be free from the fear of flying). I do this because human beings respond well to being told what to do and why.

So by giving your best performance of hypnosis to your client they will have a deep readjustment of their thinking and come out of your therapy room better. They will feel confident by being in control. When they think of the aeroplane they will be filled with excitement that they will enjoy their flying journey.

Fast phobia technique
I often use the fast phobia technique. A client will often tell you what has happened to them in a linear order. You will notice that they will begin at the point of the problem starting and finish at the

end on a bad note. With this therapy you find their safe place before the problem began, you get to the end of their story, but rather than ending on a negative point you go beyond and find out when they started to feel okay again and this is the end point you use.

Now you can sandwich their negativity with two good points of reference. Starting at the very end on the good point, you get them to tell you their story backwards until they reach their beginning again by ending up on their good point.

Do this slowly to begin with, bring in all their senses helping them by saying you can hear people talking backwards and cars are driving in reverse and so on.

You get them to do this faster and faster until they scrub off all their associated negative emotions.

After you know they can do their story in reverse you play the Benny Hill theme, this is what I use and I have it on loud, I also pop on a red nose and pretend to play a trombone. The whole event looks silly, sounds ridiculous and is funny. Once they see the funny side of this, they are pretty much better and no longer have a problem.

You do however have to have a 'temperature test point' of a number. They could tell you that their fear of flying is on a level 10 out of 10, you ask what is the lowest number they would be able to manage their problem on?

They may say a number 1 or 2 and so on each reverse you can check their 'internal temperature gauge', so you can both notice how low it is going on each pass.

My treatment plan

My treatment plan for a client is to simply complement my client's requirements.

Following our first initial contact either by phone or email I offer them a free complimentary consultation, this lasts as long as it takes. I never clock watch, either at this point or in a therapy session although if I do have music playing in the background I know how long the treatment has run for via knowing what track is playing.

I often get asked how many sessions the therapy will take and I say: "My objective is to turn you around as soon as I can by getting you better again. However everyone is different, so too are you and this depends on your mind being able to process the changes that we do."

With some therapy that I use, I ask the client to eat a high protein meal as this helps the brain function at its optimum level and process the information better. Particularly, I like children to have eaten a protein rich meal before therapy.

Once I have permission to proceed with therapy I take a history of my client to get a deeper knowledge of why they hate flying, why they have it and why is it important to them to change.

No problem is a problem so long as the truth doesn't remain hidden. I am also alert to any secondary gain a client might throw into the mix. It's important to cover any eventuality, the mind is tricky and deceitful when it wants to be, so I like to dot the I's and cross the T's.

Whilst taking notes on the client's history, I take the opportunity to start re-framing their thoughts, by getting them to look at their problem in a new way.

I like to get rid of negative baggage that a client can come with. Then once this is out of the way, I find that their trance experience is much deeper, with the quality enhancing the experience for them. For some of my clients, this can be one of the few times that they have felt completely relaxed.

Clearing out the negativity to begin with could be a Swish pattern, or Gestalt therapy. Although I will have a criteria in my head of what I will do in a session, a returning client will sometimes ask what are we doing next week. I will inform them of what to expect, however their feedback may lead me to a different course of action. I find clients can often throw you a curveball.

I have taken clients out to face a particular problem, for example taking them to the airfield and experiencing the planes.

Although this story isn't about flying, it illustrates the approach and allows me to talk about my beautiful Greyhound called Jack. I once saw a young man terrified of dogs. This was Jack's time to shine and help pay me back for all the free keep he has had. After doing the fast phobia therapy on my client, a re-framing of the problem and a transactional analysis, I brought in my dog. He was happy to stroke him and soon was feeding him. So as you can see I do different things to get my clients better.

So I've got this far, so what's next, this is time to keep-um quiet by putting them into a trance.

Once you know they have cleared out their mental rubbish then a client is only too willing to go into a deep trance. From my history notes I find out their most safe, wonderful, relaxing place they would like to be in, whether this is real place or a fantasy world.

I remember once I had a woman client and her fantasy place was Superman's bedroom . . . well there's a first for everything! Finding a peaceful place is more usually a beach or in the countryside. I bring in all the client's senses to really put them in that place. Once in an altered state, I then start to reprogramme their mind with the intentions that they came for.

Six-step-reframe
Depending on the severity of their problem with flying, I will do a six-step-reframe. This gets a client to use a different part of their makeup or psyche.

I explain to the client what I am going to do. The client will be using their dominant hand and having a 'Yes' finger and a 'No' finger, raising the one for 'Yes' and the other for a 'No'. Once the client is in a trance, you address the part that has been responsible for their negative behaviour. You get this part to talk to you via their 'Yes' and 'No' fingers.

Once you have the part willing to talk to you, and it is willing to change, you may get a positive 'Yes' finger response, all well and good. However if you get a 'No' response, you use this method like a flow chart by going back and starting over. Once you get a positive 'Yes' you tell this part on behalf of your client that they want to change, and also if this part will take on a new role or responsibility. If you obtain another 'Yes' you get that part to find three new things it would rather do instead of being fearful of that plane. This could be something they have never done before, to do something even better or to rekindle how they once were.

When this part has chosen these three new ways of thinking, behaving, and acting you then let this negative old behaviour choose just one of these that it would like to be. You future pace the client to the negative event, perhaps getting on the plane, but now they respond with the new behaviour pattern.

Once the scenario is played out, you ask the part if it was happy with the result. If you receive a 'Yes' answer you get that part to know it has two other choices to use if it wishes to in the future. You get all the parts to go back where they came from and I always do a little cheer and clap, to welcome the new part back into the fold. You can finish this off with a trance just to lock it all into place, and then bring the client back to full conscious awareness.

One client kept giving me 'No's' throughout her session, I was wondering if this will ever work on her as I didn't receive a 'Yes' answer at all in the session. So I was amazed when she got back to me a week later to tell me how much better she was and that how well she thought her therapy session had gone. I didn't think it had worked. It goes to show how the unconscious can work even after a client has left you.

Of course getting to this point can take three or four sessions on average. I also offer top-ups as the client may feel they want to get things off their chest later.

I finish off by asking the client if they have any concerns, or anything they wish to share with me. This is to end on a positive note for them. I don't tell them to call if they have a problem as they're walking out of my practice in a positive frame: they came with the problem and now it is improved. I don't want to sound arrogant or be egotistical but you have to be upbeat by having a strong belief in your abilities. You are providing your client with knowledge because anyone who wants to change is seeking knowledge. Also for the client to have a full positive experience, you have to believe in what you are doing for them believe it for themselves.

I have been in practice since 2004, and I am also a master practitioner of NLP. I also offer E.M.D.R. (Eye Movement Desensitization and Reprocessing). So I feel I have an arsenal of therapy weapons to hopefully help clients with any difficulty they bring me.

Skype is another good medium to offer hypnosis to people far and wide. I have seen clients from other countries as well as Skyping in the UK.

I hope I am a part of that person's recovery as they achieve success, happiness and confidence. So my mantra for my client is 'helping you towards success'. Hopefully, in some small way I have been able to do the same for you and I hope you will have lots of clients flying fabulously in the near future.

Finally, on a personal note would like to say a big thank you to my mentors/teachers who have been devoted in helping my personal development in hypnotherapy. Dominic Beirne and Paul Castle where I first trained in hypnotherapy also Jennie Kitching who mentored me to become an Advanced Hypnotherapist. Ann Jaloba, without Ann I wouldn't have had published work. Steve Miller for personally mentoring me, helping create my Anxiety Hypnosis brand, his assistance and devotion is second to none. Finally, my beautiful partner Christine, for putting up with me and where none of this would have been possible as her support for me has been unquestionable, Thank you my Love, Philip

Want to know more?

You can find out more about Philip's Flying Fabulously programme and get his Flying Fabulously toolkit, including help for clients when they are actually on the plane, at www.anxieyhypnosis.co.uk

You can also read his case studies, including how he helped a woman to take a long haul flight followed by an island hop in a light aircraft for her honeymoon, at yourhypnotherapyniche.com

Chapter Eight

Tinnitus, dealing with a complicated condition

Graham Parish, known as The Tinnitus Man is an expert in this little understood condition. He describes the mix of technical knowledge and therapy skills he brings to helping his clients live with tinnitus

My interest in helping people with tinnitus started when I developed tinnitus some years ago. My partner also sufferers with tinnitus, and although we are both fortunate enough to have only mild symptoms we are well aware of the enormous impact this dreadful affliction can have on a person's life.

When I first started looking for help with tinnitus I did an Internet search. Information was very sparse and of little help. I could find only one hypnotherapist completely specialising in tinnitus, and he was based in America. That therapist would only divulge his secrets if I purchased his extremely expensive training course. There were many other hypnotherapists who advertised on the Internet and offered help with tinnitus. None appeared to specialise in tinnitus treatment, they were all general hypnotherapy practitioners. I'm sure that they were all very good at their job. But when dealing with such a complicated condition as tinnitus you really do need to know what you are talking about.

So I decided to make tinnitus my specialty, my niche. I read everything I could on the subject. I learned about how the ear functions; how the sounds we hear are decoded by the brain; how the brain decides what to do with that information and what priority it gives those signals and where to send them. I learnt about the many different causes of tinnitus, and how damage to the ears plays a significant part. I also learned about different types of treatment for tinnitus. This includes CBT and Tinnitus Retraining Therapy and physical treatments such as sound maskers to hearing aids.

I researched all the physical relaxation therapies such as yoga, Tai Chi, massage, craniosacral therapy and acupuncture. I also looked at the benefits of mindfulness, meditation and self hypnosis. To this day, I still keep researching and learning about tinnitus.

Armed with all this knowledge I set about developing my own system for the treatment of tinnitus. And this what I am going to share with you; how I use a blend of hypnosis and coaching to educate my clients and help them find ways to deal with their tinnitus. I have not included any scripts with this system, simply because as you will discover each client has their own issues that need dealing with. I have found that a one size that fits all script just does not work.

Treating tinnitus sufferers is a complex task. No two clients will be the same, their circumstances, backgrounds and tinnitus will be different, as will their treatment plans.

I do not believe you can cure everyone. And I'm not sure that the word cure should be used, at the moment there is no cure for some types of tinnitus. However, we can help our clients to learn how to manage their state of mind and therefore manage their tinnitus. What we are trying to do is help them ignore the sounds they hear and push them into the background.

Two categories of tinnitus
I believe that there are two categories of tinnitus clients. The first

category is those that have developed tinnitus because of psychological issues such as depression, stress or anxiety. With these clients it is sometimes possible to 'cure tinnitus', when the causes or stressors are uncovered and dealt with, usually the tinnitus sounds subside. I am still wary of using the word 'cure' though, if the depression, stress or anxiety returns usually the tinnitus will too.

The second category is those who have physical ear damage, hearing loss or nerve damage. With these clients a cure is virtually impossible, but I can usually help them to become unaware of their tinnitus, the sounds are still there but they learn to ignore them. Again control of mental state is an important part of the treatment plan, because any return of stress, tiredness or anxiety can trigger a worsening of the tinnitus, this is often referred to as a 'spike'.

Essentially, your client has to learn to ignore their tinnitus, and by helping them to remove the stress and anxiety from their lives they can do that.

With the right techniques you can help the majority of clients that present for tinnitus treatment, anything that you do that helps them to cope with their tinnitus is a success story, so keep that in mind as we take a look at a simple explanation of tinnitus.

What is tinnitus and what are its effects?
First and foremost, tinnitus is not a disease and sufferers are not ill. It is a psychological condition that people can, with the right help, easily learn to become habituated to.

Tinnitus is without doubt an awful affliction. Many tinnitus sufferers have become used to the sound of their tinnitus and have just learnt to live with it, they have habituated to it. And whilst they may experience spikes in the severity of their tinnitus, on the whole they have come to terms with it.

These are the lucky ones, if luck is the right word. But there are others that are having a truly dreadful experience every day of their lives. Their tinnitus noise is constantly there, day and night, and often in their words 'drives them mad'. Their tinnitus has such a severe effect on their life, that they cannot function normally. They cannot go out socially, go to work or even have quality leisure time. That noise is there all the time, there is simply no respite. It affects their quality of life.

Tinnitus is invisible. From the outside tinnitus sufferers appear completely normal. Those who do not have tinnitus simply cannot understand how debilitating this affliction is. Even friends and family can sometimes forget that the sufferer is experiencing severe discomfort.

They may even fail to appreciate just how depressed or anxious the tinnitus sufferer is. How difficult it is for them to sleep and how this can make them short-tempered or angry and difficult to live with. So building understanding, support and compassion from friends and family is very helpful.

Where does the noise come from?
Science is still trying to work out the whys and wherefores of tinnitus.

New discoveries are being made all the time, but as yet there is still divided opinion about the exact causes and mechanism of tinnitus. Perhaps this because no two people experience the same noise and there are many ways this awful affliction can be contracted.

From a medical point of view tinnitus is widely viewed as a psychological condition. By definition, the noise that tinnitus sufferers hear cannot be heard by another person, the noise cannot be heard externally. The noise is an internal representation of sounds experienced only by the sufferer.

There are other types of tinnitus that we don't have the scope to cover here, where the tinnitus can be heard externally and these have usually got an associated medical condition.

Many scientific experiments have been carried out that confirm that even those who do not suffer from tinnitus hear sounds if they are confined to a soundproof room and have only silence for company.

The brain is programmed to listen for sounds, it's the brain's way of protecting us, keeping us alert for any signs of danger, listening out for anything that could harm us and threaten our survival. The brain has to hear something, anything. Silence is not an option.

So when there is complete silence the brain starts to zero in on even the smallest sound in an effort to hear something. Some researchers believe that what you hear when there is complete silence is the sound of the electrical activity in your brain.

The mechanics of hearing

The workings of your ears are very complex, and there are many good books or Internet resources that will explain this in greater detail. But here is a short explanation:

When a sound travels into the outer ear, the air pressure of the sound waves moves the eardrum.

The eardrum is connected via three small bones to the inner ear or cochlea. Sound energy entering the cochlea via these bones causes a membrane in the cochlea to vibrate. Rows of tiny cells, called hair cells, sit on this membrane and vibrate according to the frequency of the sound.

These hair cells convert that movement into electrical activity and send electrical signals, via neural pathways to the auditory nerve and then on to the brain, which then interprets those signals as a noise. The brain matches those noises to stored sounds in the memory and tries to make sense of them.

The sounds that can be recognised are dealt with accordingly. A good example of this is when you hear your name.

However some sounds are not recognised or are interpreted as being a warning of danger. This unrecognised or suspect information is also passed to our limbic system which is also responsible for our emotions. These emotions can activate a part of our autonomic nervous system which is responsible for our fight or flight reactions.

This all happens outside of conscious awareness in a split second and is part of our inbuilt survival system and hardwired into our brain. This reaction to sounds that are unknown may be perceived as a warning of danger, and is there to protect us.

What is thought to happen in the case of tinnitus sufferers?
When hearing is damaged in some way or there is a lack of sound signals to send to the brain, the brain has no signal to interpret. The brain searches for something to hear, to fill in the gaps. It increases the sensitivity of what it can hear.

It amplifies the sounds that it can hear, and that can just be the electrical activity in the brain or the ear, it can then transmit that sound to be processed by the auditory system.

This electrical activity is always present in the background, but because it is not normally considered important it is filtered out in favour of more recognisable sounds.

An often-used example of this filtering is when someone points out the noise of a ticking clock in the room. This is a noise that you were unaware of until it was pointed it out to you. And now your attention has been drawn to it, you can't but help listen out for it; until something more important draws you attention away from it.

Now the brain is consciously hearing this unknown background noise, it has been brought to the brain's attention like the ticking clock, and the more the brain hears it the more importance it gives these signals. The limbic system picks up on this and perceives this constant background noise and starts to see this noise as a threat.

It is not long before the autonomic nervous system becomes involved and the flight or flight response kicks in. Adrenaline is produced and as a result people become more alert and start to feel anxious, blood pressure rises and they begin to breathe faster.

The noise has now become a big part of awareness. If a person reacts badly to the noise their brain begins to recognise the noise as even more of a threat, something to be aware of and it amplifies the noise even more. Once anxiety or panic about the noise sets in a vicious circle starts to take effect.

You can probably see the cycle developing, the more the noise upsets the person, the more attention is paid to it, stress and anxiety increases and more adrenaline is produced. The person will now concentrate more on the noise and so it goes around and around getting worse and worse.

And all this happens simply because one of the functions of the auditory system is to warn and alert to danger. It is a completely natural reaction to what is perceived as a possibly dangerous situation. This is why keeping your client's anxiety and stress levels down to a minimum is vitally important in the management of their tinnitus. Anything that produces the fight or flight, adrenaline response will affect or spike their tinnitus levels.

What causes tinnitus to start in the first place?
The causes of tinnitus are many and varied and can be linked to many things such as:

- Physical trauma, such as a car accident, mugging or broken bones
- A major emotional life changing event, such as divorce or bereavement
- Surgical procedures
- Major dental operations
- Drug use, aspirin and some prescribed drugs
- Hearing loss, loud noise, ear infections or syringing
- Severe impact to the head or jaw
- Chronic worrying, anxiety, depression and stress
- Overwork, tiredness and over-exertion

I find that many of my clients have suffered hearing damage due to exposure to excessively loud noise in their younger years.

The tiny hair cells in their inner ears have been damaged and they have suffered some degree of hearing loss. In other cases clients have presented with tinnitus and the cause has been linked to excessive stress or traumatic events which have affected them psychologically. Others may suffer as a result of taking medication which has damaged their hearing.

No matter how it started, the likelihood of it going completely is quite rare unless there is a treatable physical condition or it is purely psychological.

And until a cure is found the best that many can hope for is to be able to manage the condition, to learn to fade the noise into the background by concentrating on other things. This is known as habituation.

My treatment programme: a three-pronged approach
My programme consists of a three-pronged holistic approach that works in the following areas:

Area 1. Getting the right medical treatment
Area 2. Living a healthy stress free lifestyle
Area 3. Maintaining a healthy mindset

So let me explain these areas one at a time to help you understand in a bit more detail just how this programme can help your clients.

Area 1 getting the right medical treatment This is probably the easiest to deal with because it concerns any existing or future prescribed medication and advice.

My programme is a complementary therapy and I strongly advise that your clients should continue following any medical advice that they have been given, and keep taking any medicines they have been prescribed. Please ensure that they continue to follow the advice of their physician, they are treating any physical symptoms and are best qualified to make those judgements.

tinnitus

I am assuming here that your client's medical professionals have ruled out and or dealt with any issues such as earwax blockages, tumours, fluid in the inner ear, problems with the TMJ, (temporo-mandibular joint) or jaw alignment issues, and that they have been referred to an audiologist and have been diagnosed as suffering from tinnitus.

They should also continue to use any hearing aids and/or sound maskers with which they have been issued. Please ask them to continue with any Tinnitus Retraining Therapy or CBT they are currently receiving.

Remember we are working alongside and complementary to their current or future tinnitus treatment. Anything that helps them to cope with their tinnitus is of benefit.

Area 2. Living a healthy stress free lifestyle. This section of the programme is concerned with the many and various areas of your client's life that could have an effect on the severity of their tinnitus symptoms and include areas such as diet, smoking, alcohol, stress, anxiety and exercise.

Working closely together, you need to identify where your client can make adjustments to their lifestyle. Help them to make positive changes about how they live their life and understand the positive consequences of making that lifestyle change. The client needs to realise that those changes can make the symptoms of tinnitus less intrusive, effectively helping them to turn down or ignore the noises they hear.

Let's go into a bit more detail about those areas where changes can make such an enormous difference.

Diet is very important. It may well be that certain foods can make the symptoms of tinnitus worse. Keeping a food diary is an excellent way to identify these foods.

Once identified these foods can be excluded from their diet, helping the client avoid making their tinnitus worse. Smoking can be a contributory factor in not only making tinnitus worse, but also contributing to high blood pressure and other serious health conditions. The nicotine in cigarette smoke causes blood vessels to dilate, increasing the blood flow and pressure in their veins, this increased blood flow is thought to be associated with the whooshing or rushing sounds sometimes heard by tinnitus sufferers.

Alcohol has been identified as another area where control of consumption can be a factor in turning down the volume of your client's tinnitus. As with the nicotine produced during smoking, alcohol also causes blood vessels to dilate and increases blood flow.

Excessive alcohol intake can be a sign of a stressful life and is often used as a relief strategy, and it works well for some people some of the time. But wouldn't it be better and healthier to deal with the stress?

Exercise is always good for your client. It gets them moving. It helps them to be more active, fitter and healthier. There are also benefits when it comes to their tinnitus as well. It is thought that exercise benefits them not only in a physical sense, it also helps to make them stronger mentally too.

Even if that is just to get them to move around a bit more, because by moving their body they also change their state of mind too. Even just getting up and going for a short walk is enough to make a difference, who knows they might find that will help them forget to listen to the sounds in their head, because they are so absorbed in what they are doing!

High blood pressure is in its own right is a very dangerous condition, in addition, reducing blood pressure is thought to help in tinnitus noise management.

A major area where a client can make changes here is to reduce salt intake. With all the other lifestyle changes they make, like reducing stress and anxiety levels, and taking more exercise, the client can reduce not only the tinnitus, but high blood pressure as well.

Stress is well known for making tinnitus worse, whether that is work stress, stress at home or just a generally stressful attitude to life in general. Identifying and dealing with stress is very important. Coaching your client to come up with solutions to remove stress and anxiety from their life is one of the most effective things you can do to help them.

Once they start to recognise the early signs of stress, and the reactions their body has to stress, they can start to change their thought patterns, their behaviours and their emotions to respond differently. They can then effectively train their mind and body not to respond to the stressors that worsen their tinnitus.

Area 3 Maintaining a healthy mindset This is possibly the most important part of the programme, helping your client to develop and maintain a positive mindset. With a positive mindset you can achieve almost anything and the world looks like a much nicer place.

Your mindset or how you think and feel about things is what drives your responses, and ultimately your emotions, and having tinnitus can be a highly emotional experience for many sufferers.

Stress and anxiety about their condition can lead to a client experiencing some quite strong negative emotions, ranging from despair and anger, to feeling depressed and even suicidal. These feelings can be brought on by the smallest of problems and at the time when a client is feeling stressed, that small problem may feel like an insurmountable mountain.

Once a client learns how to see the reality of their situation it simply becomes far easier to deal with, sometimes that mountain was a molehill all the time, the client just didn't see it that way at first.

And it's learning how to deal with these emotions that is very often where the simplest and most profound changes can be made. Using hypnosis and coaching techniques you can help your client to learn how to deal with the stresses and strains of everyday living, without magnifying them into huge problems.

These new calmer reactions to stress and anxiety can be

hardwired into your client's subconscious mind so as to make them something they do automatically.

A typical treatment plan
As I have stated before an average tinnitus client does not exist. However, there is a protocol that I follow. I normally see a client for six, weekly sessions, and if required I offer the option for monthly or quarterly top-up sessions afterwards.

One of the problems with asking someone if their tinnitus has faded into the background, is that they immediately try to listen for it. And guess what. They find it, and tend to bring it into their awareness making it seem worse.

I have found this to be a common problem, and that after a session the tinnitus is usually more noticeable. This awareness fades though after a short period of time. So it is important to not to try and 'cure it' during the session. Just let time do its work afterwards.

My conclusion is that six sessions is enough and then just see what happens. More sessions can be arranged if required, but the client needs to learn to forget about their tinnitus and get on with their life. Constant sessions will just remind them that they have tinnitus.

I have learned not to ask about how the tinnitus is after the session, it just reminds the client that they have it.

Session 1
One of the first things I do is take a detailed case history. I ask:

1. When did their tinnitus start?
2. What caused the tinnitus?
3. What is the loudest the noise has been out of 10?
4. What is the lowest the noise has been out of 10?
5. Rate the noise now out of 10?
6. How does it affect life? (Anxiety, depression, insomnia etc.?

7. What they have done so far to try and cope with it?
8. Have they been diagnosed by a competent medical professional to rule out physical causes?
9. Are there any stressful circumstances to their life?
10. Do they smoke? Drink excessive alcohol or caffeine?

As I have mentioned earlier, by talking about their tinnitus your client will be placing their attention on it, they will be listening for it, it may well make it worse which is just the opposite of what we want them to do.

There is a choice of action here, either you can say nothing and just let the client deal with it, or you can warn them that they may be more aware of their tinnitus, and reassure them that this unwanted effect will fade away after a short while.

You are damned if you do and damned if you don't! It just depends on your style and the individual client.

In my experience of working with tinnitus clients they need to have a good understanding of what tinnitus is, and how the noises they hear are produced, this goes a long way towards helping the client learn how to manage their tinnitus and get on with their life.

If they don't know how the noise is produced in their head (and most clients don't) explain it to them, so that they understand that tinnitus is not a disease and is not an illness.

Explain that millions of people worldwide have tinnitus. Only about 1 per cent of those affected have life-altering symptoms, and most learn to cope in time. Assure them that they will too. Especially with your help!

I have put together a short Powerpoint presentation that I show my clients, it contains videos and slides explaining all that they need to know about tinnitus, that way I make sure that I don't forget anything.

Next, I ask my clients to keep a food and drink diary for the next couple of weeks. Noting down what they consume every day and also how they rate their tinnitus that day. It is surprising that some foods and drinks can spike tinnitus, and by keeping a diary it becomes easy to spot the culprits and cut them out. The next task is to find out what is stressful or causing them anxiety in their lives, this is what needs to be dealt with first. Stress and anxiety will make tinnitus worse, many clients think it is the tinnitus that is causing the anxiety, usually it's the other way around. Once identified, coach the client to find ways to make changes, so that they can be calmer and more relaxed.

Finally I will induce hypnosis and deliver a relaxation script, this can be any standard script that suits the clients situation, just adding words to the effect that "the tinnitus that was so distracting earlier today will begin to fade into the background, and will be a signal to you that you can lead a more peaceful life, spending more time relaxing, concentrating on what you are doing, being more and more mindful at all times . . ."

I will also give them a recording of this hypnosis session to take away and play everyday.

Session 2
Recap on session 1. Then check

- Have they got a better understanding of their tinnitus?
- Have they kept the food diary and have any triggers been identified?
- Have they played the hypnosis recording?

It is important to ensure that the client is taking steps to make changes to their lifestyle, to deal with their stressors. They need to be taking action to change.

Next, I induce hypnosis and investigate what if anything is behind the tinnitus, then deal with whatever arises, clearing the emotions and the like.

This is of course very specific to the client, and as an experienced hypnotherapist you will have your own ways of dealing with this.

tinnitus

I use S.P.A.D.E. as a guide to work from:
o Stress
o Panic disorder
o Anxiety
o Depression
o Emotional problems
Once the S.P.A.D.E. symptoms have been worked through you will often find that the tinnitus has been reduced or in some cases gone completely. Again I will give a short relaxation script, modified to whatever we have been working on and give the client a recording to play until the next session.

Session 3
Recap on session 2.
As well as the questions from the last session ask:

o In what ways have they been feeling better?
o How has the noise reduced?
o How has the stress or anxiety been better?
If you need to do more work with the issues from the last session (S.P.A.D.E.) then this is the time to do it. In this session, I introduce them to the concept of mindfulness, and teach them how to be mindful; a very useful skill for anyone, not just those with tinnitus. Again finish with a personalised script of your choice and give the client a recording to take away

Session 4
Recap on session 3 and ensure that progress is being made. Again if you need to deal with any issues from the S.P.A.D.E. symptoms now is the time to do it.
I will usually induce hypnosis and use parts therapy at this stage. Instead of a relaxation script, I teach the client self hypnosis and give them a recording to take away so that they can practise until the next session.

Session 5

This is really just a repeat of the previous session, making sure you have dealt with any issues and the client is making good progress. I will reinforce the self hypnosis and test to make sure that they can do it on their own.

At this stage I may ask them to personalise their tinnitus. Giving it a name or personality can make it seem far less threatening. It can be used as a warning sign that something is not right. If their tinnitus spikes they need to be aware that something is making that happen, and action needs to be taken to resolve whatever is at cause.

Session 6

Recap on all the work they have done on their lifestyle, self hypnosis and mindfulness. Ask them to look back on how far they have come and notice all the changes they have made. If anything else needs to be dealt with then now is the time to do it.

I will give them a relaxing Mind Massage to completely chill them out and give them a recording of that to take away.

I wish them well and remind them that I offer monthly or quarterly refreshers to keep them on track.

Want to know more?

You can find out more about Graham's work at www.thetinnitusman.co.uk and download his "3 tools to help your clients cope with tinnitus". You can read his case study, where he describes how he helped a long-term tinnitus sufferer by, amongst other things, creating an avatar for each ear at www.yourhypnotherapyniche.com

the hypnotherapy experts

Chapter Nine

Manage, control and abolish anxiety

Dan Regan has built a very successful practice by helping people to manage and then control their anxiety. He explains how he uses hypnotherapy and NLP techniques and the positive effect his approach can have

In their 2014 report, *Living With Anxiety*, the Mental Health Foundation suggests that almost one in five people feel anxious all of the time or a lot of the time. And most of us have noticed that people are more anxious today than they were five years ago. There can be no doubt that anxiety and panic disorders are particularly prevalent in today's society, with some commentators even describing this as the 'Age of Anxiety'.

As someone who suffered with social anxiety for over 20 years, I know first hand how unpleasant the overwhelming physical and mental symptoms of anxiety can be. I also know the lengths to which sufferers are capable of going, in order to hide their anxiety from others and to avoid or withdraw from uncomfortable situations.

No matter what the specific circumstances that lead an individual to struggle with anxiety in their life – for example, particular ways of thinking, learnt behaviour, attitudes, beliefs, behaviours or the stresses, worries and demands of modern living - they are most certainly not alone in their battle with their anxiety.

Most people will have at some point experienced a degree of nerves, worry and anxiety, perhaps before a big test, exam or presentation. Yet for others their anxiety, whether generally or in relation to something specific, reaches a level where they can't function or do things they want to. They may even avoid certain things altogether to avoid the possibility of feeling bad again.

And whilst anxiety is a normal human reaction, designed to keep us safe in the face of threat, for many people it reaches a crippling level where they feel they can no longer cope.

As anxiety is so common, it's pretty much guaranteed that, whether you are aware of it or not, you know several people, who under the surface, are battling their anxiety.

Research by scientists for the University of Cambridge, University of Hertfordshire and Imperial College London, published in 2013, suggests that about 18 per cent of the UK population have an anxiety disorder, costing the country nearly £10 billion a year. It's a similar case in the United States, where according to the National Institute of Mental Health; the same percentage of the adult population is struggling with an anxiety disorder.

Anecdotally from what my clients tell me, it is likely that the true figure is even higher and that anxiety levels are under-reported, as many anxious people may not readily disclose how they are feeling to others or seek help.

Indeed, many seem to be highly adept at putting on a 'public face' and continuing to function whilst hiding successfully what is truly going on beneath the surface. Many sufferers worry about what their boss or friends might think, the impact on their future careers or that somehow they will be perceived as weak, should others become aware of their anxiety.

As well as those with general anxiety, there are those who need help with panic attacks, OCD, phobias and fears. In addition,

abolishing anxiety

anxiety and panic can impact on other conditions. Many clients who approach you for help with other issues may need help in dealing with their anxiety as well. Anxiety can often be linked with, and be a key component of, depression, stress, sleep problems and confidence/self-esteem issues, to name but a few. Clients may also be using alcohol, comfort eating or smoking to try and alleviate their anxiety and worry.

Whatever the exact numbers of those struggling with various forms of anxiety and panic, there is certainly a large pool of people seeking help and for whom an expert anxiety hypnotherapist is the best option. This makes it a great niche to develop.

The rewards of abolishing anxiety
In my opinion, there are few things as professionally rewarding as helping someone to overcome their anxiety and panic. They may walk into your practice on edge and anxious; a bundle or worry, agitation and fear.

Whether it is something that has affected them for months or even years, it has now reached a level where it causes severe discomfort. They are very likely to be anxious about feeling anxious which, of course, becomes a self-reinforcing cycle.

They then leave a short while later feeling calm, confident and in control. Generally you may notice they seem to look physically brighter and lighter, and the way they talk has changed from fear and avoidance to possibility and opportunity.

In some cases you may help them to do the thing they have been worried about and often avoiding for years.

For example, recently I was contacted by a client who had failed her previous four driving tests due to nerves and was feeling panicky about failing her forthcoming test. After we worked together, she breezed through her next test calmly and confidently, passing it easily. She is now enjoying the freedom to be able to go places and do things, without relying on others.

In other cases, clients may feel they actually have their life back – as though you have helped spare them from a life sentence of anxiety. They can now move forward in areas such as relationships, their career and in their social lives. I received a text recently from a client with whom I worked over two years ago and who had just been promoted for the third time because she was no longer anxious at work and had found her voice.

Another recent client had been virtually housebound for over six months due to his anxiety and panic attacks. He is now anxiety-free and enjoying going out with friends, finding work and doing the things he wants to do.

About anxiety
When resolving anxiety, knowledge is power for a client as they shift away from viewing their anxiety as something that has control over them and rules their life. Recognising that everything they are experiencing is part of a natural survival mechanism designed to react to threat and stress, provides a level of reassurance that change can be achieved.

All of the physical sensations, emotions and thoughts are natural reactions to stress and threat, but right now they are happening in an overwhelming way that leaves them feeling unable to cope.

Before they understand what anxiety actually is, they may have been concerned that there was something seriously wrong with them, which of course added to their worry levels.

Whilst in the grip of their anxiety symptoms, they may have rushed to A&E or called for an ambulance. And even having been checked out and told it is anxiety and panic, they can still be worried about feeling that bad again or have a persistent niggle at the back of their minds that something must be wrong with them.

To help start to alleviate this, I will always explain to a client about anxiety; what it is, why it starts and how it becomes a habit that keeps re-enforcing itself. Their mind is overprotecting them, responding to perceived and imagined psychological stress and worry as if it was something life threatening where they need to be ready to take action to protect themselves. All of their physical sensations such as breathing faster, sweating and shaking are there as their mind gets them ready to take action instantly. Yet the truth is that in this day and age there is rarely anything life-threatening to fight or run away from.

Whilst anxiety and panic can strike after a specific event, for most clients it is a delayed response to a highly stressful period in their lives. In many cases they will have been dealing with those stresses, events and changes and seeming to be managing effectively, only to find that when things quieten down they start to struggle with anxiety and panic.

I will explain that it's like a tipping point where there has been so much internal worry, anxiety and stress that their mind goes onto high alert for potential threats of danger.

They then start imagining the worst or talking to themselves about how bad things will be and create the anxious feelings. The more they focus on those worst case scenarios, the more they prime themselves to feel anxious, both while they imagine it and should they find themselves actually in that type of situation.

I will often use the analogy of a car alarm. A car alarm is useful if someone does try to break in to your car, but if it is over-sensitive and goes off when someone just walks past then it is set too high and is no longer being helpful, in fact it is a thorough nuisance, except of course when it needs to ring to keep the car safe.

It is also useful for a client to understand about pattern-matching, that is the way our brains use memories and experiences as the reference material or template for how to respond in similar future situations. If their brain matches their current situation to one in the past where they felt anxious or panicky, then those emotions and feelings of dread and fear can start at the detection of a perceived threat before they even have a chance to think about it.

I will often talk about how our memories are like documents on a computer. Sometimes we need to open up, amend and resave them as a new version without the attachments, (that is the emotions), present.

And as with all anxiety, because it is something that a client has learnt to do, they can unlearn those patterns or update them. And that's when they can start enjoying feeling happier, calmer and more confident.

How hypnotherapy can help: two-pronged approach
From working with my clients, I have found that hypnosis and NLP techniques are ideally suited to helping clients abolish their anxiety.

A client who comes to see you stressed, worried and on edge can soon learn how to feel calmer and more in control. They can learn quickly ways that will enable them to change their thoughts and feelings day-to-day whenever they choose. Instead of their anxiety running them, they learn how to take back control.

In essence, using hypnotherapy and other techniques, I help my clients learn how to get freedom from unnecessary anxiety using a two-pronged approach:

First is learning to *manage* anxiety. This means that they can turn down their anxiety level to an appropriate level for what they are doing or experiencing at that time. I will often use my hand to demonstrate that their anxiety is at the top of a scale and can be brought down as they learn to manage it.

Second is learning to *control* anxiety so that it can be 'switched off' when it is unnecessary. I visually turn my hand like I am flicking an imaginary switch from on to off whilst talking to clients about this. I believe that a key cornerstone of success with anxiety clients is having this dual approach both in sessions and in the tasks set for them to put into practise outside sessions. Essentially you are helping them get to a stage where they have learnt to manage and control any anxiety they experience so that they no longer need help now or in the future.

I help the client understand that our minds can't tell the difference between something we imagine vividly and something that is real. To do this, I may teach the client techniques such as dissociating from imagined worst-case scenarios, spinning feelings, and changing their critical/anxious internal dialogue to something less impactful. This empowers clients and builds up their robustness to cope with stress.

Clients have learnt how to generate their own anxiety through their internal thoughts so I am helping them discover that if something is going on inside them (whether it is images, self-talk or feelings) then they have the power to control and change it, they just didn't know it until now.

Because it is so effective, I teach every client the 7/11 breathing technique and instruct them to do this several times a day. I may also have them do some mental counting techniques to interrupt the pattern and have them switch their focus from anxiety and worry to what is going well in their life.

I also let them have a copy of my rapid relaxation hypnosis audio and teach them self-hypnosis so that they can regularly feel more mentally and physically calm.

When we first meet, clients will often tell me that their anxiety means they never switch off, their brain is always in overdrive and they can't ever relax. So often the first step is helping them realise that, in fact, they can feel calm, relaxed and in control.

Using hypnosis, they can shift from focusing on the anxiety, to imagining how they want to think, feel and react. It's about a change in focus and creating a new association. I encourage the client to feel calm and in control whilst at the same time thinking about those things that used to make them feel anxious going well.

I may use timeline therapy to clear out the emotion of fear, whilst retaining any positive learnings. The fast phobia cure is useful for dealing with memories that are acting as reference material in similar current situations.

In essence, anxiety is an unhelpful misuse of the client's

powerful imagination which generates those anxious thoughts and feelings. Linked to this, is the unhelpful pattern matching which means we tend to respond in a similar way in similar situations.

Our job is to help a client recognise that anxiety is a normal, natural response that is firing off when it isn't needed because their mind is overprotecting them in response to a perceived or imagined threat. We must then unravel the pattern of their anxiety and start to interrupt it so that our clients can then run new, more helpful, patterns that move them towards what they do want.

Treatment planning
Every client is very different in terms of the context in which they experience their anxiety and what they want to achieve from working with me. Usually, I will work with someone for six, one-hour sessions.

Ideally, I like to see clients weekly initially and give them tasks in between sessions to reinforce and complement our work in session. Once we have created some positive momentum, we will increase the gap between sessions to maybe two or four weeks. This helps the client realise that over time and in more situations, their previous anxiety and panic has gone.

Whilst I may use certain processes, structures and techniques in my work, I base the content of each session on the particular needs of the client in front of me rather than using scripts or 'one size fits all' approaches.

Free initial consultation
I will always encourage a client with anxiety to come and meet me before we start the process. They may feel worried about the process and what it may involve or be anxious about finding the office and so it it is helpful to get those things out of the way early on.

This consultation gives them a chance to meet me in person, learn more about what I do and ask any questions before deciding to go ahead. I want them to feel comfortable with me and what I do before we invest in the process.

At the initial consultation, I will ask them to tell me a bit about what they are experiencing right now and how their anxiety is impacting on them. I will then link this when explaining how anxiety works, how it keeps itself going and how I help people.

In many cases, a client will tell you that you are their last hope! They may have tried prescription medication, over-the-counter products, self-help resources and other therapy before they come to see you. Whilst none of these impact on our success, I like to have an awareness of what they have already tried, to know what has or hasn't helped in the past.

I know some hypnotherapists will keep an appointment slot free straight after a free consultation so that if the client wants to go ahead they can start there and then. Personally, I don't do this as my appointments are in demand and I don't want a gap where I could be helping someone else. In addition I don't want my clients to feel pressured, obligated or 'bounced' into paying for a session, but this is just my personal preference.

Session One
In our first session working together, I will take a full case history from my client. I want to understand what is going on with their anxiety and how it manifests itself – what are they thinking, feeling, and doing in respect of their anxiety? What is it stopping them doing? How is it a problem?

Many clients start to feel better simply from getting it all out and talking to someone who understands anxiety. They may have been churning over and dwelling on these things for months with no one to talk to and no release. Just talking about it, and starting to understand what anxiety is, can often be a vital step on their road to success. We will be looking for any previous events that may be relevant to how their anxiety started and that contribute to the ongoing anxiety and panic.

For many clients, a series of stressful or worrying events have led to their anxiety. It can be useful to know what was going on in their lives in the six to 12 months before their anxiety started. There may be certain ways of thinking and beliefs that contributed then and still impact now.

For others, there may be specific past events, memories or mistakes that still generate an emotional response now when they think back to them.

I like to have an awareness of how they think about these (not necessarily the detail which may still be distressing) and the level of emotion they can still generate. If needed, during our sessions we can make sure that the emotion on those past events is detached, which changes the pattern-matching response so they can now behave and respond in a more helpful way.

Whenever someone is getting a consistent response in terms of feelings, thoughts and behaviours there is an internal pattern being run. Our own beliefs, experiences, values, perceptions, and ways of thinking come together like ingredients in a recipe to produce the anxious response, the pattern of anxiety. Once you help a client change the ingredients, or change the order of them, they get a very different end result.

So in particular during the first session, I am looking to identify the pattern that keeps the anxiety going. How are they doing their anxiety habit? They are likely to be imagining anxious, worst-case scenarios, running a stream of negative, anxious self-talk and also experiencing the classic physical sensations (feeling on edge, restless, sick, hot, sweaty etc.).

I will spend some time understanding which of these they are most aware of. For example, if they are imagining worst case scenarios and then feeling anxious, I will ask them about how they do these. Do they run them associated or dissociated? Black and white or colour? Bright or dark? Life size, bigger or smaller?

By understanding their pattern of anxiety you can target the techniques you use in sessions and teach your clients how to do them when they are on their own.

I always ask the client about other aspects of their lives such as stress and worry, any previous history of anxiety or depression, any impacts on their sleep and how confident a person they consider themselves to be.

In essence, I am exploring all the pieces of their unique anxiety jigsaw. This helps me to understand what may be a cause or a symptom of their anxiety which influences the content of sessions and can often give helpful indicators of progress when reviewed in future sessions. For example, in a future session we may review whether their sleep improved because they are worrying less, whether they now feel more confident in social situations etc.

I work to help a client reach a solution state. I always ask my client about what they want to get out of the sessions.

Often they will just say something along the lines of, 'I want to stop feeling anxious all the time, and stop worrying about irrational things' or they may say, 'I just want to feel normal'. I never let them get away with this! I like them to be much more specific in what they want to achieve and how they will know they have achieved it. And I make sure they are focusing on what they do want and not what they don't want.

As things improve for them, a client's expectations of what may be possible may well increase beyond what they initially hoped for. I always use their initial goals as a benchmark for where they are now in each subsequent session.

I believe that giving clients specific tasks to carry out in between sessions is vital in helping them learn to alleviate their anxiety.

One task that I give to every anxiety and panic client is 7/11 breathing. I tell them to do it regularly throughout the day, even if they don't feel anxious at the time so that they become very familiar with it. Other tasks may include:

- Going for a daily walk (keeping their eyes up)
- Thinking of three things every morning they are looking forward

to that day and, at the end of the day, three things that went well that day
- Listening to a relaxation hypnosis MP3 track
- Specific techniques they have been taught to dissociate from imagining anxious scenarios or to change negative self-talk.

All of these tasks help the client to learn how to manage and take control over their anxiety more and more effectively.

Session Two
In the second session I will carry out a review of what has been happening since we last met. I will ask the client about their anxiety, check on progress and make sure they are implementing the tasks we agreed at the previous session.

I may teach them additional techniques they can easily apply themselves such as removing the emotional intensity from imagined worst-case scenarios. For example, I will ask them to think of one of those things they have been imagining that makes them feel anxious (e.g. an upcoming event) and to scale (on a scale of 1-10) the level of anxiety they feel as they think of that scenario.

I then ask them to change the sub-modalities, for example, by stepping out of the image, moving it away, shrinking it right down and so on. I then ask them to again rate their anxiety level and make further changes if necessary. Often, as they think of the situation I will get them to ask themselves, 'am I just making this up in my head?' and if so suggest that they make up something they would rather think about.

Recognising that they can change the scenarios in their head, rather than just trying to distract themselves from them, gives a client a powerful tool they can use and puts them more in control over their thoughts. If it is in their head then they can change it, especially once they recognise that they are just making it up.

In this second session I will also do some hypnosis. Before we start I explain what it is and how they are likely to feel. Often anxiety clients say they can't relax or their mind never switches off so the hypnosis sends a powerful message that in fact they can feel calm and control their thoughts.

My approach is to help them to focus on moving from where they are now to how they want to be. For example, I may have them see themselves on a screen and then add in positive beliefs, behaviours and resources and then see themselves going through their daily situations having these. I then have them step into that version of themselves and imagine feeling calm, confident and in control as they mentally rehearse things going how they want them to do. I will also do plenty of future pacing.

As a large part of anxiety is using their imagination in unhelpful ways, they can soon start using that ability yet in a more positive, helpful direction.

Subsequent sessions
Subsequent sessions tend to follow a similar pattern, linked to a client's individual progress:
o Review of progress since previous session – what has changed?
o Check for any changes in other areas of their life such as sleep and stress.
o Review use of techniques they have learnt and tasks agreed.

I always ask the client to rate on a scale of 1-10 where they are now (with 1 being where they were when they contacted me and 10 being how they want to be doing things).

The session itself would then depend on progress to date and may include teaching them additional techniques and tools to control anxiety. There would also be some hypnosis, NLP techniques or timeline work designed specifically around where the client is now.

Want to know more?

You can find out more about Dan and get his complimentary anxiety-busting e book at www.danreganhypnotherapy.co.uk. Read Dan's case studies at www.yourhypnotherapyniche.com

Part Three

Nicheing in weightloss

The field of weightloss is growing as obesity levels continue to rise. It is a busy field where therapists compete with or work alongside other professions. Some of the most successful practitioners in this area are specialising with one particular group or providing a special mix of skills. Here are three of the best to describe what they do.

Chapter Ten

Man up lose weight: a male perspective is different

Ex-boxer Daniel McDermid has built a very successful niche helping men who want to lose weight. He gives this programme a distinctly 'macho' feel which, as he explains, helps him work with his client as a team

Britain is bulging. If you're not overweight yourself, it's likely you have some fat friends, some portly pals or some chubby chums. Wobblers, you might have noticed, are everywhere. We've become a nation of fatties. So just what is going on?

Are people happy to be fat; content to heave around huge, trouser-busting bellies; joyous at being jiggly?

I doubt this very much. There are those, of course, who are in denial – people who don't accept that they are, in fact, fat and fewer still who will admit to being actually obese. In the case of men, a popular delusion is that XL stands for excellent and is evidence of mighty warrior genes. They believe they're big lads – just one solid lump of muscle with a modest coating of fat to keep them warm in winter.

They like their beer, they like their food and they're not going to change their attitude for anyone. Not even themselves, it seems. Then there are those – and there are plenty of them who do recognise they're at least a little overweight and might possibly benefit from losing "just a pound or two." Of course, they're often shocked when I tell them bluntly that they need to shed five stone (or whatever the figure might be).

My *Man Up Lose Weight* programme is a recent addition to a wide range of services I offer at Leeds Hypnotherapy Clinic and complements my other more general weight-reduction course. As the name suggests, *Man Up Lose Weight* is targeted at men with the aim of appealing to that proportion of the population which it might be argued is resistant to more conventional therapy.

A brief wander about any UK town or city provides enough evidence of there being a huge potential market for such a service for men. Although distinct from the fitness market, my programme's main competitors are gyms and similar institutions, to which men are instinctively more likely to turn to once it dawns on them they need to do something about their weight. This explains why the *Man Up* site has a definite 'macho' feel to it, though in essence the treatment is built on the same solid foundations as my other programmes, combining cognitive behavioural therapy with clinical hypnotherapy. The success of the programme is centred on the appeal of a highly-ranked website that has evolved using all the strategies available in website construction with great emphasis being placed on continued updating and monitoring.

There are a number of important reasons why the men who come to me need to lose weight. One might be vanity. This is psychological and more complex than is sometimes recognised. I explain the psychological benefits of being thinner at greater length in my forthcoming book *Man Up, Lose Weight: It's a Doddle*. but here it's enough to say that, by nature, people like to look good. It is human nature to make value judgements based on appearance – it's why people put on party clothes or dress up for an interview. Of course, the psychological benefits of being slim overlap with the physical benefits, contributing to an individual's overall well-being.

There are also obvious physical advantages of being an ideal weight. Illnesses associated with obesity include: various types of cancer; heart disease; high blood pressure; Type 2 diabetes; early ageing and early death. Great benefits of weighing less include being able to join in activities that are otherwise challenging, if not impossible, including many sports, dancing and, perhaps, even sex.

Given such facts, it seems unlikely that anyone might wish to remain fat when presented with the opportunity not to be so. And the truth is that most folk would choose not to be so. They would prefer to be slim, even if they claim they're happy as they are.

Then, why is it that so many people remain obstinately overweight. Clearly, something isn't working. The food industry hasn't helped with hidden sugars and trans-fats, the proliferation of takeaways, supermarket offers, ready meals and so on.

But my notion is that what is not working is the collective attitude towards weight. With so many fat people about, the condition goes almost unrecognised by many, or is even regarded as normal. Meanwhile, many others might be aware they are fat but are convinced that losing weight is a hopeless dream, or at best a daunting and miserable challenge.

But I know this needn't be true. Few people understand their condition properly, which is why one of my tasks is to explain it to them clearly. I work to make overweight people leaner, fitter and happier and my *Man Up* programme, is specifically targeted at men.

I've helped hundreds of people achieve a healthy weight without them resorting to surgery, without them adopting weird diets or signing up for punishing fitness programmes and without them purchasing overpriced gimmicks or pricey 'miracle cures'. I help clients to re-evaluate their hard-held beliefs about weight loss, challenging their conditioned thoughts. I teach them that achieving a healthy weight and maintaining it can be easy. It doesn't matter how much has to be shed – with my help and with the benefit of hypnotherapy any individual who decides he or she wants to be lighter can achieve a healthy weight whether it's just a few pounds or 10 stones that needs to go – or even more.

I am now going to explain what I do to help. If you decide to practise in this area this is what you need to know.

At this stage, I'd like to state that I don't hate fat people. Being fat doesn't make someone a bad person. In fact, some of the kindest, most empathetic, wittiest people I've known have been way overweight.

But that doesn't mean to say that it's their excess weight that is making them happy, or witty and, to be sure, it is not doing their health a lot of good – psychologically or physically. If they are honestly pleased to be fat, then fair enough – they have that choice. Anyone can stay fat if they want to (so long as they eat enough food, of course). I teach people to be aware and to recognise that they have a choice. I teach them that people can change. I know that people can change.

I treat clients using principles of cognitive behavioural hypnotherapy (CBH) and rational emotive behavioural therapy (REBT). I employ a structure of treatment that I have developed, inspired by the pioneering work of American psychotherapist Albert Ellis, aimed at helping people achieve emotional responsibility. My treatment for weightloss clients also follows some of the principles of my friend and fellow UK hypnotherapist and weightloss expert Steve Miller.

Much of the advice I offer people wishing to lose weight is based on motivational principles. At the clinic I am able to integrate these principles into the unconscious mind of a client using hypnotherapy skills and techniques. I also provide clients with an insight into self-hypnosis and offer further help here through a download from my website.

The efficacy of self-hypnosis very much depends on the individual, though it is only fair to point out that hypnosis induced by a trained therapist is likely to be more effective. At the clinic, inducing a trance state and then using techniques adjusted to suit the particular client forms a basis for treatment.

So how does my weight-loss programme work?
One starting principle is that I speak truthfully. And that means fat is fat. It's not my intention to be rude or even provocative by saying that, even though I know a lot of dieticians, nutritionists, health specialists and doctors are reluctant to employ the F-word. They're worried, I imagine, of being accused of causing offence. So, if other people prefer to use euphemisms to describe the condition that is their decision. But fat is still fat no matter what you want to call being overweight: amply cushioned; big-boned; a bit on the large side; portly; a little stout; well-built; generously proportioned; comfortable . . . the list seems endless.

The first question I ask a client is: does he accept that he actually is fat? Under the circumstances, this might seem a daft question bearing in mind that they have booked an appointment based on this very issue. But perceptions are a significant part of treatment. It is important that a client is aware that they are indeed fat and by how much and that they are in need of assistance to achieve a healthy weight.

At my clinic, we start with a weigh-in so that both the client and I can agree what the starting point is. I also tell the client that if he doesn't already own a pair of weighing scales himself, buying some should be his next job after the first session. Sometimes the individual weighs more than he likes to admit – but that is not an issue – I'm not being judgemental. The client then tells me how much he would like to weigh and then I tell them what he needs to weigh, which also lets him know how much he needs to lose. Occasionally, our figures tally but usually it comes as a shock to the client when I tell him exactly how much fat I am expecting him to shift.

I now ask the client what he hates most about being fat –

in other words why does he want to be slim? Answers vary. Some clients say that they just want to be healthy, some say they can't abide the thought of being unattractive to the opposite sex, others go much further than that. For me, gleaning this information provides a useful insight into the client's psyche which is going to help me anchor that driving force of motivation in the client's subconscious when we eventually progress to the hypnosis stage of treatment.

At this stage I chat with clients about the importance of embarking on the programme in a positive frame of mind. The programme lasts for six weeks from the initial consultation. I stay in contact on a daily basis, usually by text message. I meet with the client every week and this involves a weigh-in, discussion of progress and continued motivation and usually a further session of hypnosis to help ensure resolve is not waning.

The programme is based on the simple principles of awareness and the obvious truth: *Consume fewer calories than you burn off and your weight will fall.*

But the programme is not a conventional diet plan. It is about the client accepting responsibility. There is no point in blaming other people or other factors for being fat. No food is banned and treats are permitted. This is part of the 80/20 rule – the client being coached to eat healthily for 80% of the week and being able to eat a bit of what they fancy for 20% – a principle championed by weightloss expert Steve Miller.

I persuade the client that the whole programme is something to look forward to and something to enjoy. If the client has been a dieter before, he can say goodbye to that merry-go-round of fat – diet – depressed – eat – fat – diet – depressed – eat . . .

The programme is based on an authoritative approach and positive reinforcement is delivered in my daily contact with clients. The client recognises he is in control of his own body. I am there to support him.

During the initial consultation, I get the client to either explain to me or write down a list of reasons why he thinks he is fat. The list will vary from client to client – some will write: "diets are boring" and others will write "I have a low metabolism" – but one of the most common reasons cited is "I eat when I'm stressed and I'm stressed a lot."

I look at the list and then get the client to tear it up. Each and every point is an excuse unless he has written down "I'm fat because I eat too much."

I'll take as an example one of those excuses – metabolism. The word seems to me to be a favoured one within the diet industry. But it is little more than a distraction, a contrivance even. However, because of its pervasiveness, it needs clarification. Your basic metabolic rate (BMR) represents the minimum energy required to carry out normal functions. Muscle cells need more energy than do fat cells and it follows that men, in general being more muscular than women, burn off more calories than do women. It follows then again that, in general, men are designed to consume more calories than women on a daily basis. It also means that muscular men such as body builders and professional athletes have a higher BMR than your average bloke as their additional muscle cells are using more energy. But fat people also tend to have a high BMR because they need a lot of calories to maintain those fat cells. The good news is that a fat person is going to burn more calories doing the same exercises as someone who weighs a lot less.

The important fact to note, however, is that when differences in body sizes and body composition are taken into account, energy expenditure is notably similar among all individuals.

So forget about metabolism. The message is No More Excuses.

But what about stress? Surely stress is well known to be a cause of overeating and comfort eating? Again it's no more than an excuse, but again it warrants explanation.

The reason people sometimes turn to food to ease stress is that anxiety releases an adrenal hormone called cortisol that triggers, among other things, food cravings. It is part of your body's natural defence system. In addition, it is known that eating encourages serotonin levels in the body to rise, which produces a feel-good factor, even if the feeling is short-lived.

So stress is a factor in overeating? No. Stress is just another *excuse* to overeat. It is *not* a reason. By blaming stress for being fat, the individual is denying responsibility.

One alleged source of stress that afflicts the majority of those caught in a cycle of anxiety is actually being fat. He's stressed because he's fat and so eats and becomes fatter and more stressed and so overeats and so the cycle continues. Well, overcome the weight problem and the cycle is broken. Simple.

But that seems a bit straightforward to many people. It's not uncommon, then, for someone to claim that there are other sources of stress in their lives that they need to sort out before they are going to able to lose weight. And this is where it begins to get a bit more complicated. For reasons of space I am unable to fully explain the reasoning behind this, but details can be found in my book *Stop Smoking: It's a Doddle* (misunderstandings regarding anxiety/stress are a precursor to smoking) and in my forthcoming book *Man Up, Lose Weight: It's a Doddle*. In short, the theory is that all anxiety except innate fear is self-fulfilling. Anxiety breeds anxiety. The good news is that this can be dealt with effectively through cognitive behavioural therapy and hypnosis.

The lesson is that nothing on this planet can cause us anxiety unless we allow ourselves to harbour fear. By being assertive, and grasping the responsibility to take matters under control we can eliminate anxiety. It is often a simple matter of training the mind (through trance if necessary) to think logically. It is why phobias can be overcome; it is why obsessive compulsive disorders can be treated.

To return to the immediate issue of weight loss, I teach my clients to be aware of what they eat. As I say, nothing is banned from the menu. It is up to the client to grasp responsibility. I provide him with the tools to do so, including motivation.

Of course, some people know more about the kind of meals they eat than others. For this reason, I provide them with guidance on the healthier options they can choose and include menu plans and cooking tips for clients (in association with professional chef Raphael Ganet). I also remind them that if and when they feel hungry, not to worry – it's unlikely they're going to starve to death any time soon. The time will soon arrive when not feeling full is no longer a signal for the belly to cry out for an immediate top-up, but becomes a positive signal that the programme is working.

I also include in the programme other conventional tips and advice for clients, including the fact that thirst is often confused with hunger – a mistake that can usually be resolved with a glass of water. I encourage clients to keep a weightloss diary and to place Post It notes around their environment to remind them of their wish to be slim and to maintain their motivation.

There are also 'negative motivators' that can prove useful in treatment, such as the client keeping a picture of himself at his fattest by his side at meal times to serve as a reminder as to why he wants to eat healthily. If necessary, I can use aversion therapy under hypnosis to treat a client who has a condition, for example diabetes, where they need to stop eating unhealthy food immediately. In such a case it might be appropriate to make the man think that chocolate tastes like faeces, but in most cases I consider such treatment to be too extreme and prefer motivation techniques.

One popular technique is to encourage clients to imagine themselves at the weight they intend to become and for them to adopt the confidence and body language of someone of that weight. The client is often surprised by the positive effect it has on his thinking and outlook.

I also offer advice to clients on exercise. Though my programme is not primarily based on losing weight through exercise, I encourage clients to raise their activity levels as the fat falls off. This usually happens naturally, anyhow, with the client happy to become less sedentary. Within my programme is advice on a range of physical activities that might appeal – the important thing is for the client to choose something he enjoys rather than something that seems like a chore and will become demotivating in the long-term. Sometimes a client will be so taken by his new, lighter physique that he wishes to take exercise to higher levels and even become super-fit. In such cases, I use my contacts to help him find suitable trainers or instructors.

By offering continued support, I ensure that none of my clients lapses back into their former overweight selves. Maintaining his ideal weight once it has been reached requires no more than the client eating and drinking appropriately. On occasions when his weight might go up a little, over Christmas for example, I coach him to readjust. Using the techniques learnt during the programme soon puts matters right. I tell him: monitoring one's weight on a regular basis means that you keep in control. You are in charge of your own well-being.

Treatment Plan for the average *Man Up Lose Weight* client:
The client and I will be a team. We will work together to build a strong mindset and provide the motivation to help him let go of harmful habits and embrace healthy practices. These new patterns are designed to ensure he loses weight and maintains his achievement in the long-term. It should be noted that this particular programme is not suitable for clients with epilepsy or a history of psychiatric illness. If a client is clinically depressed (within the medical definition of the condition) I will ask him to consult his GP before accepting him on the programme. This programme is not designed for those in a vulnerable position. Humour plays a significant part in the programme. It is a fun programme built on serious foundations.

How to run a programme like this: what my clients receive
We will work closely together for six weeks to increase control over the client's eating habits, build his motivation and to focus and recondition his mind and lifestyle so that he loses weight from day one and continues to maintain control of his weight in the long-term. This six-week period includes daily support from me with one-to-one communication, either by text or conversation on the phone or by email. The client can contact me for support and reassurance at any time of the day. The programme also involves a series of face-to-face sessions to help the client manage his dietary portions, eat better and maintain his motivation; I provide sample menu plans based on the 80/20 rule. This means the client can lose weight without being restricted to a boring, demotivating diet.

The face-to-face sessions involve motivational straight talking as well as hypnosis and homework-based tasks. There is great emphasis placed on accepting responsibility which includes abandoning excuses – my client will recognise he is unable to fool me and that there is no benefit either in trying to fool himself.

We will discuss and resolve any personal difficulties and challenges that emerge as the course progresses. Honesty is a key word in the programme – clients are expected to be honest with themselves and with me and I will be honest and straight-talking with the client.

There are terms and conditions that I operate, all of which I make clear to the client at the outset of the programme and the client and me sign a contract prior to the course commencing.

Weight-loss is measured weekly and a reasonable, achievable target set for the following week. Clients declining to reach their pre-agreed target will be taken off the programme and given a pro-rata refund. No refund will be issued to clients who leave the programme of their own volition before its completion. Pro-rata refunds are calculated on the number of face-to-face sessions or weeks remaining. It will occur to many readers that this process, in itself, provides motivation and the occasions I have felt compelled to expel a client from the programme have been very rare.

The six session overview
First Session: Setting the context and building foundations (90 minutes)
I establish a rapport with the client and offer a further explanation of the authoritarian nature of the programme. A case history is completed and I explain how hypnosis works. We then conduct the excuse-busting exercise.

A current photograph may be taken and emailed to him. This will be used for homework. Foundation planning also includes 80/20 meal plans.

The typical client will be encouraged to use Post-it notes in the kitchen, to buy a pair of jeans or suit that he will fit once he is slimmer. I will then conduct a session of authoritative hypnosis – usually based on an alert-focused state of trance.

Out of trance, I speak with the client and we agree the homework action plans and the client repeats to me what he is going to do so that I am able to see that he has fully understood the undertaking.

Second Session: Changing the client's internal tone (75 minutes)
We start with a weigh-in to check how much weight has come off and we review the homework set in the previous session. I teach the client how to conduct self-hypnosis with an authoritative tone and identify motivational strategies.

He learns how to change his internal tone to an authoritative *Man Up* tone. He practises the self-hypnosis until I am convinced he is competent enough to try it at home and I extract a promise that he will do so. If the client likes music, I will get him to pick an up-beat track that will become his motivational theme tune. This record is an anchor for the slim and healthy man he is going to be. He will hum this to himself when faced with challenges so that he remains focused. Together we identify three motivational strategies to use over the following week to complement the 80/20 plan.

Third Session: Formal tailored authoritarian hypnosis session (60 minutes).
We start with a weigh-in, then review homework. This is followed by a tailored authoritarian hypnosis session conducted by me, with emphasis on taking back control over food and exercise.

Now the client has lost a significant amount of weight and is already feeling healthier, I introduce the proposition of increasing his exercise, bearing in mind such factors as age, needs, preferences and the like. The most common proposal at this stage is for the client to walk more frequently and over longer distances. We consider a 7-day menu using the 80/20 plan.

For homework, I tell him to observe the behaviour of fat people he sees. How they eat, how they move and the like. This is to make him more aware of what habits he should be avoiding.

Fourth Session: Tailored motivational and authoritarian hypnosis session (60 minutes)
The usual weigh-in is followed by the review of homework.

I then conduct a tailored authoritarian hypnosis session, with a strong emphasis on the client being in complete control of food. He will transform the part responsible for his unhealthy eating habits. A new motivating action is introduced, which will be part of homework along with motivational self-hypnosis.

Fifth Session: Tailored authoritarian hypnosis session (60 minutes)
Weigh-in followed by the homework review. I then conduct another tailored authoritarian hypnosis session. This one is to reinforce the client's resolve and confidence and introduce more motivational action plans, which might be as simple as stepping up the walking.

Sixth Session: Tailored authoritarian hypnosis session and action plan (60 minutes)
Weigh-in followed by review of homework, followed by tailored

authoritarian and motivational hypnosis to reinforce everything that has been learnt in the previous five sessions. Together we identify and agree on the essentials of the client's long-term action plan. The client is now well on the way to achieving his ideal weight and I give details so he can keep in touch. I tell him there is a follow-up free session available to be arranged at an appropriate date. All that remains is for me to congratulate him, wish him well and express my confidence that he will achieve his goals.

Your guide to delivering a *Man Up Lose Weight* authoritarian and motivational script

The following techniques should be delivered in an authoritarian voice. A deep voice is an advantage, otherwise a strict tone should be adopted. This reinforces the 'no nonsense, no excuse' approach to losing weight which will help you motivate and empower clients, in particular male clients.

Before beginning to induce a trance, I write down what I am going to say and anticipate delivering it with controlled authority – it is a metaphorical slap across the face – a no-nonsense wake-up call. I write down every excuse the client has given for being overweight.

I also write down what my client may think about all the negative connotations associated with being overweight. Here are a few likely statements:

- People think overweight men are lazy
- People think overweight men have no willpower
- People think overweight men are unhealthy
- People think overweight men are unattractive

If your client is a father, make him consider what his children think of him being overweight. If he is a grandfather, make him consider that he might deny himself the opportunity of seeing them grow up. Then get him to consider the health consequences of overeating:

- Cancer
- Diabetes
- Heart disease
- Early ageing – wrinkled skin
- High blood pressure
- Anxiety

The list goes on. I want my clients to begin to hate fat for what it has turned them into and what it is doing to them.

When you are ready to induce trance, have your client sitting straight with his head held up high. Trance will be induced using an authoritarian technique. Do not use a relaxing permissive technique. It is useful to use an induction that will get your patient to realise something is happening quickly. You are working with his beliefs.

Count him down from ten to one, however unlike relaxation meditative trances, this will be a focused trance, delivered in a very deep booming voice. You can find an example script at this book's website yourhypnotherapyniche.com. I hope you have found this useful and I wish you the best if you go into the much-needed area of helping men to Man up and Lose Weight.

Want to know more?

Daniel's weightloss programme is among a number of services he offers at his clinic in Leeds city centre.

His forthcoming book, Lose weight: It's a Doddle *is due out soon. You can get his complimentary guide* Eight Expert Slimming Secrets *by visiting his website at www.manuploseweight.co.uk*

To get a copy of Daniel's motivational script, go to www.yourhypnotherapyniche.com

Chapter Eleven

"I build confidence and clients lose weight"

Rosalind Smith is The Weightloss Witch. She uses personal experience to develop a weightloss programme in which she helps her clients change their mindset and lifestyle

My story
I have worked as a hypnotherapist since 2003 and am the author of the weightloss book, *Your Road to Change*.

Even though I now have a good relationship with food, and am slimmer than I ever was, and fitter and healthier this has not always been the case. I was chronically ill as a baby because of a wheat intolerance and my parents were told to check absolutely everything I was consuming. Throughout my school years I was reasonably okay, but my stomach was very sensitive and easily irritated. Going into my teens I developed a poor relationship with food, you could call me a 'typical teenager' who would reach for convenience foods: chips, pies with tomato sauce, sausage rolls, chocolate, crisps and anything I could eat on the go along with excessive amounts of bread.

At 17 years old I decided to move in with my husband, whose relationship with food was quite frankly worse than mine, and I knew something needed to be done, so I decided to cut back on some of the stodge 'junk' to help both of us. I still wasn't overweight, but knew this would have been a downward spiral for both of us if drastic action wasn't taken. I was unable to completely cut out all of the stodge, and now realise that these were my comfort foods.

This pattern continued through into my teens and whilst having my children. When I became pregnant with my first child this tapered off but I was still eating the same 'junk' foods. After having my second child I was then diagnosed with IBS (Irritable Bowel Syndrome) and was told to do a food elimination diet to find out what the triggers were.

They were wheat, gluten, dairy, caffeine, certain fruits and vegetables, but this still didn't stop me from eating them. I used to get angry with myself because I knew the foods that triggered me, all the foods I loved, were the things I need to cut out. I ended up craving them even more, it was a total mystery to me why I was craving the things that were causing me much discomfort.

I tried every fad diet going and would regularly lose half a stone within the first week, only to put the weight all back on again and more, because I knew I would be able to lose it all again quickly. It was almost like I was telling myself that, 'I've achieved that, you've done it now', so I would start eating again and the weight would pile back on leaving me in despair as to why this kept happening. I found myself in a never-ending cycle of guilt and yo-yo dieting.

I had all the knowledge and information and knew exactly what to eat and what exercise I should undertake, but I just couldn't get my head into gear. I convinced myself that this was my natural weight saying in my mind: 'it's okay to be chunky'; 'it's okay as long as I'm happy.' Reflecting back, I realise how miserable it made me. At this point, I began going through periods of feeling light headed, being lethargic, shaking and feeling like I was going to black out. I had several diabetes tests all of which came back clear. The GP told me it was an exaggerated form of hunger. I now know

confidence and weightloss

that this was caused by all the sugar from the refined carbohydrates I was eating.

Now at the age of 42, I have the knowledge and the understanding that I was comfort eating. I now know I was filling a void. I had to ditch the excuses and stop blaming my husband for not taking the necessary action, when it was actually *my* lack of willpower and motivation to get fit and healthy. After all it was about me. It was at this point that I decided enough was enough, I needed to make a change and I started at the gym once again.

I remember sitting on the beach in America with my iPhone researching all about fitness. I was practising weight loss hypnotherapy at this time, and getting remarkable results, mainly using the hypnosis gastric band, but I felt something was missing, I needed to do something 'extra' and to be more involved with my clients and certainly needed to do the fitness just for me. Little did I know at the time that I would soon be training in a gym five days a week, two of them with a personal trainer, and training with my husband and children for the remaining three.

I wanted to find a way of being more involved and encouraging with my clients, which would enable me to give them extra support. I felt I needed to be fulfilled too and make my work more enjoyable. Then I could show compassion and empathy and give my clients the clarity that they need.

Because I'd been through it all myself, I had worn several of the t-shirts! In fact I could put them in a platinum frame and hang them in my office.

I took action and things changed for the family. Since my husband joined the gym he has lost five and a half stone and I have lost two. How amazing is that? Our eating habits have completely changed, going from the oversized portions and the stodge, we now eat small regular meals consisting of lean meats, fish, vegetables, nuts, wholegrains, and fruit. We still enjoy meals out. I honestly would never have believed that I could enjoy food as much as I do now, but eating the right foods makes all the difference. This has taken a lot of discipline, determination and focus but it's absolutely worth it.

I have a true understanding of how people can have a really unhealthy relationship with food, and now I do my very own fitness videos, something I never dreamt was possible. This was never in my radar.

My education still continues through research regarding fitness and nutrition as it always will. I am having a career that is my lifestyle, you can't get any better than that!

I really love the fact that I can pass on all the knowledge and experience that I have. I can tell you, hand on heart that the last 12 years it has been a hard slog. Many times I felt like giving in, but somehow I managed to get through any negative thoughts and remain positive. I make lists of all the positives attributes that I could give to others, to lead a healthier and fitter life. I am open with my clients as and when I feel it necessary, this gives them an insight into my own weightloss journey.

What I tell my clients
I am very clear with my clients about the world we live in and how this affects what we eat and our weight. When it comes to a healthy diet, balance is the key to getting it right.

This means eating a wide variety of foods in the right proportions, and consuming the right amount of food and drink. Portion sizes nowadays are much larger; it seems over time people have lost the knowledge of what healthy eating and exercise is all about. We now live in a fast-paced society, with convenience and processed foods which are full of chemicals, sugar, fat and salt plus other ingredients that our body just doesn't recognise, and which contain no nutritional value whatsoever. Anything that comes in a packet or has a sell-by date on it, are usually bad for us. Going back to basics and 'eating fresh' produce as much as possible is what our bodies crave and thrive on.

When we think back to our ancestors, their eating habits were completely different to what they are today. They would cook from scratch and processed foods weren't readily available. They would have eaten off the land, and grown their own vegetables, food was used as fuel to maintain bodily functions, whereas today food is taken for granted, and used more as a coping mechanism or as a tool and a pleasure. We celebrate everything with food.

I tell my clients: "If you are not used to eating a healthy diet that promotes your well-being, then making gradual changes to get you started will be helpful in sustaining long-term success. For example, you can drink water instead of high-calorie juices and sugary drinks, and switch from full-fat to low-fat dairy products. Selecting lean meats instead of fatty cuts and wholewheat grains instead of refined grains, and eating wholemeal pasta, wholemeal rice, (another healthy alternative is Quinoa) can lower your intake of unhealthy fats and increase your dietary fibre intake."

Adopting a nutritious, well-balanced and a healthy-eating lifestyle, along with physical activity, is the foundation of good health. Healthy eating includes consuming high-quality proteins, carbohydrates, heart-healthy fats, vitamins, minerals, and water in the foods you take in while minimising processed foods, saturated fats and alcohol.

Eating in this manner helps you maintain your body's everyday functions, promotes optimal body weight and can assist in disease prevention; stopping diabetes, high blood pressure, lowering cholesterol and much more.

The nutrients in foods support the activities of day-to-day living, protecting cells from environmental damage and repairing any cellular damage. Protein rebuilds injured tissue and promotes a healthy immune system. Both carbohydrates and good fats fuel the body, while vitamins and minerals function in support of the body's processes. Vitamins A, C and E, for example, act as antioxidants to protect the cells against toxins, and B vitamins help extract energy from food. Calcium and phosphorus keep bones strong, while sodium and potassium help to transmit nerve signals.

Without a healthy eating plan, any of these essential functions might be compromised and that can have a profound effect on mood and sense of wellbeing.

As research shows, a lot of our processed food these days contains an awful lot of sugar, and most people are really unaware of this because they believe what they should really be looking at is the fat content or the calorie content. For example, a 400 gram tin of soup has a total of 14 grams of sugar. The daily recommended amount of sugar is 90 grams, so when purchasing single items ensure the sugar content is no more than five grams per 100 grams. I warn clients to be aware of anything that's fat free, (labelled 0% fat or similar). These could be full of sugar as many manufacturers reduce the fat content and replace it with sugar to maintain the taste. Some of these labels are found on cereal bars, yogurts, and frozen meals and this is just a marketing ploy.

The brain is about 80 percent water, so it is important for us to drink lots of fluids for it to function properly. We lose about 2.5 litres of water each day through our sweat, breath and urine, and in order to replace the water we have lost, we should drink 1.5 litres of non-alcoholic fluids every day. (The rest of the water we lose is replaced by fluids in the food we eat and by chemical reactions in the body). If we don't drink enough fluid, this can affect our mood and concentration.

As well as the benefits of eating well it is important to understand the benefits of undertaking daily exercise, this helps to promote weight loss and has a myriad of other benefits. Among these are an overall healthy body and healthier body systems.

The body systems that benefit during exercise are many and include the cardiovascular, respiratory, and skeletal muscle systems. Exercise will promote lean muscle mass. In addition to this, lungs and heart will become more efficient, making it easier for oxygen and essential nutrients to be delivered throughout the body. Basically, exercise will make it easier to perform daily activities that the client may currently find troublesome. This alone is why exercise should be an important part of a weight loss plan and be daily. Also, I tell my clients that not only does exercise help us to lose weight and keep it off, but it also has other important benefits such as:

- It boosts the immune system, helping fight illness and infectious diseases, from colds and 'flu to cancer, diabetes and osteoporosis
- It gives strength, suppleness and endurance as well as more energy for physical tasks like gardening and housework
- It makes the client a better lover, with more energy, a higher libido, greater endurance, a lower risk of impotence or other sexual problems
- It boosts confidence and assertiveness and makes the client look better and younger, and feel more positive
- It relieves stress and, because of the endorphins (the 'feel-good' hormones) it releases, it improves mood and can help beat depression

I warn clients to watch out for the mindset which believes that because they are working out in the gym, they can indulge in cakes, pastry and the like. I tell them that the calories contained in just two biscuits could take a good 40 minutes to burn off.

The mindset
Understanding food and the benefits of exercise as I have set out above is essential if you are to offer a successful weightloss programme. You also need to have an understanding of the psychology behind people's eating habits: it isn't as simple as just encouraging an individual to eat healthily and going on a restricted diet.

Just to give you a brief understanding of how the mind can

influence eating habits this is an overview of how it works.

There are two different kinds of mindsets, the *Growth* mindset and the *Fixed* mindset. People with a *Fixed* mindset believe that their basic skills and qualities are more or less set from birth and there is not a lot you can do about it.

They adopt the attitude of: 'its okay for him/her, he's/she's brainy' or 'he's/she's clever.' If they are not good at something from the word go then they don't see the point in putting in the effort to learn it. In contrast, people with a *Growth* mindset believe that most things can be achieved through hard work, practise, commitment and by not giving up when things get difficult. They know that people might be particularly talented at certain things, but recognise that for them, this is just a starting point and that even these people need to work in order to improve on their talent.

There is a difference in behaviours between people of each mindset. (You can find a diagram of each mindset at the website to go with this book).

In the *Fixed* mindset, intelligence is seen as static, and people will avoid challenges and give up easily when faced with obstacles. Effort is seen as fruitless and useful negative feedback is ignored. These people feel threatened by the success of others and as a result they will tend to plateau early in their lives and not achieve their full potential.

In the *Growth* mindset, intelligence is seen as something which can be developed, and these people will embrace challenges and persist in the face of obstacles. Effort is seen as a path to mastery and these people will learn from criticism. They will find lessons and inspiration in the success of others and as a result will reach a higher level of achievement.

Do I believe that a client's mindset can be changed? Absolutely, *Yes*!

The mindset is just the programme that's been running a long time and has become a habit, but that habit can be changed, right now, to anything or run any programme that you want. It's about adopting a positive mental attitude. This also means it's imperative to live in the present moment and leave the past in the past, if you keep focusing on negative memories and drains, that will prevent you from moving on and reaching your goals.

I tell my clients: *The Body Can Achieve What the Mind Believes.* Even with a client with strength and willpower, that nasty little fixed mindset voice can creep in. Here are the five key thoughts that a fixed mindset can have that could sabotage efforts when trying to lose weight:

- I have bad genes, there's no way I can lose that much weight
- What if I fail, I'll be called a failure?
- I don't want to embarrass myself, people will laugh at me
- I don't have the willpower to stick with a healthy diet so who am I trying to kid
- I'm just not as smart/lucky/talented/clever as everyone else

I encourage my clients, once they recognise a fixed mindset thought, to make a choice between believing those negative thoughts or reframing them. Affirmations are always positive and here are five key examples a client can use:

- No excuses this time, I'm getting started today
- If I fail, it's okay. Great accomplishments mean risk
- Forget diets. I'll take it slowly and make healthy eating a lifestyle change
- If I don't know how to do something, I'll learn, I *can* do this
- I deserve to be healthy and have the body I desire

If your client develops a *Growth* mindset, and this is aligned to their weight and fitness goals, they will achieve success.

The client's awareness
Struggles with weight are often due to hidden emotional upset, usually the client is not aware these ever existed.

Added to this, an unbalanced lifestyle whether it be at home, work, with relationships, family, or just having stressful lives can do damage, leaving embedded triggers which can lead to comfort eating (filling a void), boredom eating and head hunger.

This is where hypnotherapy and other therapies I offer (Emotional Freedom Techniques (Tapping), Neuro Linguistic Programming, and Reiki), come into play.

These can be very useful when dealing with boredom eating. An example of this is, would be a client who says on an evening whilst they are watching television, they feel the need to occupy their hands, and they do this with food, not because they are hungry but because they are bored. Through mind-programming techniques, I get my clients to focus their attention elsewhere to distract their mind to undertake a task that is constructive instead. Another frequent issue is comfort or emotional eating. It's common for my clients to comfort eat typical examples are:

- I have had a bad day and feel tired
- I'm feeling lonely and unloved
- I feel bad about myself
- I'm upset about a comment that someone has made recently (or even several years ago)

Taking into account all of the above I can combine therapies to enable my clients to run a new programme aligned to their personal goals, healing their emotions, leaving the past in the past, and setting them free from any unwanted baggage. It also gives them a purpose filled with confidence, self-esteem and for them to be their authentic self. Once the *Growth* mindset is in place, by fuelling the mind with exactly what they need through visualisation, we can start to see profound results.

My treatment plan
The programme that I run currently consists of six sessions, but depending on how much a client has to lose they may decide to

confidence and weightloss

stay with me longer. I also run a help and support weight loss group, once a fortnight, and my clients love it.

When I start work with my clients, I make one thing absolutely clear, that this is not to be taken half-heartedly, this is going to need commitment, continuity and dedication, and this is not some sort of fad diet where you stick to it for a period of time, lose weight then revert to your old eating habits, and put all your weight back on and even more besides. I make it clear that this is a full lifestyle change that will continue for the rest of the client's life, whilst letting them know that they will be a fantastic ambassador, to not only themselves, but to their family and friends too.

I ask them why they want to become slimmer, what it truly means to them to lose weight so they recognise how important it is to be slimmer, fitter and healthier. I then ask if there's anything at all that could prevent them from becoming the shape and size they choose to be (at this stage I am looking for any excuses they might make, these could include: lack of time, too expensive to eat healthy food etc.) After we've ironed out all the excuses, taking away all the negatives and putting in all the positives,

I let them know that, if they want it enough, they will succeed. I ask about their eating habits as I need a true picture of what their eating consists of, and we decide together a course of action. This would include a new meal planner with healthy tips and advice. I explain the way to weightloss success is to ditch the word 'diet', as this signals deprivation and keeps us in a cycle of thinking about food even more and makes us miserable. We then crave the very foods that we are trying to cut down and end up on that treadmill of guilt and self-sabotage. I am in contact with my clients every day for the first several weeks to find out what they are eating.

With this support, and me taking them by the hand and ditching the word 'diet', we start the positive programme running in their mind. I make it as exciting and enjoyable as it can be as I understand first-hand all the pitfalls. It's taken me 40 years to have a healthy relationship with food, so I know what to look for. To get the client's eating in order, I then get them to follow these guidelines below:

- Limit all stodge and refined carbohydrates, these include potatoes, white pasta, white rice, pastries, cakes, biscuits, sweets as these contain refined sugars
- Make sure you eat three meals a day, eating breakfast is imperative, with healthy snacks twice daily. If you prefer no snacks then that is fine, listen to your body
- Stay hydrated, make water your drink of choice. Reduce the intake of fizzy drinks and ensure you have 6-8 glasses of fluid per day
- Enjoy at least five fruits and vegetables a day
- Choose tins of fruit in juice not syrup. (Dried fruit not included)
- Reduce your alcohol intake and stay within weekly safe drinking limits
- Cut out saturated fats found in white bread, pies, pasties, pastry, cakes and biscuits
- Use a smaller plate to serve your lunch or dinner. (Portion size is key)
- Put your knife and fork down between each mouthful
- Chew your food slowly, approx. 15-20 times per mouthful
- Stop eating when you are satisfied (if full you've gone too far)
- Do not eat leftovers, if freezable save it for another meal
- Close your kitchen at 6pm
- Weigh yourself weekly and after the first three weeks of cutting down on stodge and carbohydrates you should aim for a 2lb weight loss per week. This is sustainable long term
- Get active and build your exercise into your daily routine
- Enlist support from friends and family to help you achieve your weightloss target

confidence and weightloss

- Identify the foods you cannot live without and enjoy 'a little of what you fancy', just occasionally
- Listen to your body by following all of the above you will recognise the signals of being satisfied

Below are the key areas that I focus on to help get the client's head into gear. I say to the client:

- Set a first mini realistic goal, for example an item of clothing that's a little too tight or a size smaller. Give a time frame of when you'll be in it, and be precise
- Start planning your day from morning until night, use a diary, planner or a to-do list
- Plan your meals for the week, order your shopping online to stop impulse buys
- Start fresh and clear all your cupboards of all the junk, and keep all temptation out of the way
- Cut your portion sizes down, (dinner plates have increased in size so don't be deceived), don't leave leftovers, and close the kitchen at 6pm

Included in the programme is letter writing from the client, identifying how they felt before being overweight and how it restricted them. They then write a new letter visualising success. This could include seeing themselves slimmer, being happier, fitter and healthier.

I work with them to learn to love themselves and explain that the weight they are holding on to is just a body suit. I work with them to give the confidence and self-esteem as weight loss and confidence go hand-in-hand, both are needed to complete this programme. I then get my clients to think about the positives rather than the negatives. They adopt the following into their life immediately and they notice the difference. I ask them to:

- Start every day with a gratitude list, write at least five things that you are grateful for, this could include things like; just

having a roof over your head, food on your table, your health, family and friends, the list is endless
- Spend your time improving your fitness, eating healthily, and adopting good habits
- Spend time alone getting to know *you* better
- Believe that the world is on your side, be true to yourself
- Let go of any mistakes from the past, recognise what you have learnt from them and move forward. Life is a journey of personal development and every day is an opportunity to grow
- Look on the bright side of life
- Learn to be stronger, this way nothing will stand in your way
- Know that you can be selfish, you are important
- Understand that anger doesn't solve anything, instead just release it and move forward, affirm that you are at peace
- Loving and respecting *you* is the key to success

I enjoy working with my clients as a team and feel it's important that people get the right support to help them succeed. This is something I never experienced personally but always felt I was missing out on. I hope this chapter means you don't miss out and that it has put you on a path to being able to decide what you could offer those clients out there who need our help.

Want to know more?

Rosalind's weightloss witch programme features regularly on radio and in the press and she sees clients as far away as the United States. You can get her complimentary The Broomstick 'Get It Off' Guide *at her website www.weightlosswitch.co.uk*

To get a copy of her fixed and growth mindset diagram and to read in details about two very successful techniques she uses go to www.yourhypnotherapyniche.com

Chapter Twelve

Helping the Asian community slim down

Manjit Kaur Ruprai speaks three Asian languages and knows the damage some traditional Asian foods and eating habits can do. She uses her expert knowledge to change lives and get across the message that Indian food can be healthy

After years of working in various areas of hypnotherapy, I found weight loss of interest as I gained weight myself many years ago I knew this was due to poor eating, but it wasn't until a friend told me that I looked fat that I decided to alter my eating habits. It was my wake-up call to do something about my weight.

My friend's words seemed rude and offensive to me at the time, but I can now say that I thank him. High blood pressure, diabetes, heart disease and premature death run in my family due to years of eating an unhealthy Asian diet of fried food, with lots of clarified butter and high fats. I had to act quickly as I did not want to suffer the same fate as my family.

There is a common belief that Indian food is bad for you. The reason for this is that in Indian restaurants food is cooked with clarified butter (ghee), creams and such in order to get the right flavours. This means dishes such as korma, chicken tikka masala and butter chicken can contain about 1,500 calories per dish. This means just a main course can go over your recommended whole daily allowance and this does not even include any side dishes such as naan or rice. Foods such as poppadums, onion bhajis, spring rolls and samosas are very fattening as they are deep fried and they absorb a great deal of calories and fat during the frying process.

In the past, there has not been much emphasis on healthy eating in the Asian community and there was not much emphasis put on the health implications of having such a high fat diet. I recall growing up eating fried food and eating curries cooked in clarified butter because my family knew no better.

There is still some way to go in educating people to cook Indian food healthily. I am trying to do my bit to change this by developing the Asian Exclusive Weight Loss Programme, which is aimed at anyone from the Asian community who wants to slim down and regain a healthy body.

In recent years there have been a lot more studies which suggest clarified butter and fried food are unhealthy. Laden with fat and calories, if eaten regularly they are a heart attack waiting to happen. This has created more awareness in the Asian community. Clarified butter is pure fat and a tablespoon contains about 135 calories. Although fat has some essential properties and we need it for our body to function, ghee has a very large quantity of fat and if consumed in high quantities it is unhealthy for you.

However, even though there is an emphasis now on these risks I still see my own family members consuming fatty and calorie-laden food on a regular basis as they do not have the mindset to make the necessary changes to their diet.

Obesity also seems to be rising in India as it is following a trend of other developing countries. Unhealthy junk food and processed food has become much more accessible, following India's continued integration in global food markets. With the country developing, combined with rising middle class incomes, the number of fast food restaurants has increased, and this is increasing obesity. I have visited India several times throughout my life and have found that it has developed greatly over the past 25 years or so and still continues to develop and I have noticed that fast food is a lot more readily available, whereas years ago it was a luxury.

The truth about Indian food

However, it is not just Indian food that is unhealthy for you. The traditional English roast, fish and chips and full English breakfast contain thousands of calories per dish and are just as bad if eaten regularly.

Indian food is not necessarily unhealthy. It depends on how you cook it and the size of your portions. Like any food, Indian food can be cooked in a healthy or an unhealthy way. The nutritional values of a dish all depends on the cooking process. If you want to eat samosas and spring rolls you are better off baking them which will make them less unhealthy.

There have been recent studies that suggest Indian curries are good for you if cooked correctly as the spices that are used have medicinal effects.

Most curries are cooked with the typical ingredients of turmeric, garam masala, garlic, ginger and cumin. This is just to name a few spices that have a medicinal value. Turmeric is a common spice, used to add colour and flavour and it also acts as an anti-inflammatory and is great for healing both the inner and outer body.

Studies also suggest it is good for individuals who suffer from arthritis. According to the Arthritis Foundation, a clinical trial carried out in 2006 found that turmeric was effective at preventing joint inflammation. (The Arthritis Foundation)

Ginger is good for you, a teaspoon of ground or fresh ginger can alleviate nausea or sickness. It can also help to relieve arthritis or other joint pain. Garlic can help to lower cholesterol and helps to purify the blood. So Indian food can be good for you and it has become a popular cuisine in western culture, but it all depends on how you cook it.

In my practice I see clients of all cultures and ethnicity who struggle with weight and I specialise in seeing clients from Asian ethnic backgrounds. Hypnotherapy is also becoming popular in eastern countries such as India.

The Asian culture is very sociable with a lot of parties and celebrations taking place throughout the year, but summer is the busiest time for these social gatherings.

In the Asian culture there is a large emphasis placed around food during these celebrations. I find that clients can struggle to keep their food temptations at bay and can often over indulge, when there are so many dishes and so much food spread out in front of them. On one hand they want to eat all of the delicious food available to them and on the other hand they don't want to pile on the weight.

I recommend some simple tips to handle food during these celebrations. I ask clients to talk to themselves mentally and to keep on telling themselves that they are in control of food and that it does not control them.

This usually stops them from eating until they are overflowing. I never recommend a rigid diet to my clients as there is nothing worse than feeling deprived, I believe that this leads to bingeing. I recommend clients have one or two samosas or onion bhajis and no more, so that they feel satisfied. This is better than saying they will deprive themselves, then giving up and eating the whole plate in front of them. Another simple tip is to socialise with others, so talking and being interested, catching up on the news and meeting old and new friends, will divert attention away from food.

Some of my Asian clients are not familiar with hypnotherapy or are intrigued to know more and will ask me questions like. 'Is it black magic?', 'Will I come out of trance?' 'Will you cast a spell on me?'. To all of these questions I answer 'no', and explain hypnotherapy is not any form of mind control, no one can be hypnotised against their will and it is nothing like black magic. I wouldn't know how to do black magic!

I tell the client: "If you are unhappy with the positive suggestions that I give to you during a session you can break out of your hypnotic state. I will reassure clients that no one has ever been 'stuck' in a trance. I reassure the client that they will not be in a zombie-like state during hypnosis and they will most likely be aware of the surroundings around you. I say: "You will not be asleep and you will not be awake. You will be somewhere in between."

The language advantage
I have an advantage over other weightloss hypnotherapists in that I can speak Punjabi, Hindi and Urdu and I have an understanding with food in these cultures. I feel that clients who are not able to speak English can connect with me as there is no language barrier. When I deliver a session in another language I will often use weightloss coaching rather than hypnotherapy as this clientele is less comfortable with hypnotherapy. I find that British Asians are more open to hypnotherapy.

Regardless of culture or ethnicity most of my clients are stuck in the eternal cycle of yo-yo dieting. Some clients have lost weight successfully within a very short space of time through low-calorie diets such as only drinking smoothies, shakes or having meal replacements.

Once the typical yo-yo dieter resumes a normal diet they will regain the weight quite quickly as they are not able to keep up with the diet long term. This cycle will continue throughout their whole life unless the problems with food are dealt with and the mind is reconditioned to make healthier choices with food.

Learning not to diet
I find that one of the major causes of not keeping weight off long term is dieting. Most individuals want a quick fix and fast results so they end up on a diet. Then they will complain of feeling hungry most of the time, feeling deprived of the food that they enjoy, become bored of eating the same food, feel frustrated with weighing themselves constantly and not having the willpower, self-belief and motivation to succeed.

A dieter will never be able to keep up with the diet long term as they will deprive themselves of real food that they enjoy and will soon become bored, leading them to go back to their old self-destructive ways of not having any self-control.

Most of my clients will have tried every diet under the sun before they come to see me. In my practice, I do not teach my clients to diet, deprive themselves or deny themselves of real food. It's not about the black and white thinking of either being on a diet, or eating for England. It's all about having a sense of balance. I will go back to basics with my clients and teach them that everything is good for them in moderation. It is likely that no one will have told them this before.

I myself have been on diets in the past and have become bored and hungry, so they lasted no more than two days and then I ended up caving in. There are definitely no quick fixes to weight loss as I cannot wave a magic wand and make the weight go away. I do not ban 'naughty' food as after all we are all human and need a treat every now and again whether it is cakes, crisps, onion bhajis, samosas or drinking a glass of wine.

One of my clients Inderjit, used to eat two chapattis twice a day and then binge on biscuits and cakes, but through hypnotherapy I was able support her to recondition her mind to eat smaller portions and not binge, but to have a little treat every now and again. This way she did not feel deprived. Another client Julie used to eat three packets of crisps a day and was very unhappy about her weight, but through hypnotherapy I was able to re-condition her mind to make healthier choices with food so she now only eats one packet of crisps a week. I teach clients to eat everything, but with a sense of balance.

I teach clients that weight loss is all about facing up to your food demons and stopping the excuses that keep you overweight, so rather than eating the whole biscuit tin, have one or two to keep you satisfied and fulfilled. This is better than not having any at all. Then human nature kicks in, you will hate the deprivation and you will eventually rebel against the denial. Weight loss is all about having the self-confidence and belief that you can be slimmer and healthier without being on a diet. Weight loss is all about taking control of food and learning to stop it from controlling you. Once you learn to take control of food, weight loss will be much easier to achieve and maintain as you will have reconditioned your mind to make better choices with food and eat everything in moderation long term.

Hypnotherapy is a great tool for weight loss and in this deeply relaxed state, I am able to support clients to tap into the subconscious mind to change behaviour patterns with food. The subconscious mind is like a huge filing cabinet that stores all pleasant and unpleasant habits, emotions and visual images, but it is not immediately accessible. We tap into it through hypnosis so that we are able to change behaviour that we no longer want. Hypnotherapy uses the power of positive suggestion to bring about change to thoughts, feelings and behaviour that are stored in the subconscious mind. So, hypnotherapy for weight loss is about supporting the subconscious mind to make healthier choices with food, to exercise and to motivate you to achieve a fabulous, healthy body.

My treatment plan
The Asian Exclusive Weight Loss Programme works well for my Asian clients as they can still enjoy the food that they usually eat, but I guide them on how they can make it healthier and to eat less

of it. For example they can bake samosas in the oven instead of frying them, as with frying they can absorb a high amount of fat and calories. They can cook curries in a non-stick pan using oil which is much better than cooking in butter or clarified butter which makes it fattening and calorific. It is best to avoid rich fattening creams and to use tomato based sauces, which are much healthier. If a rich creamy sauce is wanted, it is best to use light and low fat creams than full fat. These few simple tips can make a great difference to your health and weight.

Clients who come onto my Asian Exclusive Weight Loss Programme receive six coaching sessions which can be combined with hypnotherapy, but it is optional as not all clients are open to being hypnotised.

The sessions last approximately one hour and can be delivered in Hindi, Punjabi, Urdu or English. Over the course of the six weeks, the client receives full support throughout their weightloss journey in the form of an SOS service: they can contact me 24/7 if they feel a binge coming on or are struggling with food. They receive daily personalised text messaging support to monitor their progress or I can have a Skype or telephone chat with them if they require it. The client is given weekly motivational tools to manage their food so that their enthusiasm remains sky high. An example of a motivational tool is hanging up a smaller outfit and letting the client visualise getting into it once they have lost the weight or they might want to stick warning signs up where there is food temptation. In addition all clients on this programme are added onto my secret Facebook support group where they receive continuous support from myself and others.

With continued support, my clients are able to achieve their desired weightloss goals and are able to transition into a new healthier way of eating as I recognise that weight loss can be hard to achieve if you don't have the correct mindset and support. This programme works well for my clients and they know that I am there to encourage them and monitor their progress every step of the way and give them a good kick when their motivation is slacking.

My clients like a straight, yet friendly and positive approach as they want to be told what they have been doing wrong over the years to pile on the weight. When they are going off track they like a firm approach as it helps them to get their focus back. Most of my clients have tried fad diets and popular slimming clubs before they come to see me and they know the soft approach hasn't worked on them.

Session 1
Session one sets the scene of the programme and involves the client taking ownership of their weight gain as I find that clients that make excuses and blame everyone else are quite difficult to work with.

Usually the client is 'excuses free', as by this time they will have accepted that it was their lack of self-control and motivation which made them pile on the weight. I will explain to the client what is involved over the course of the six weeks and how we will work together as a team to achieve weight loss.

The client is made fully aware that I have a direct and straight-talking style and excuses are forbidden and should weight loss not be achieved week on week I will boot them off my programme.

This sets them a challenge as they will not want to fail themselves. I feel that a wishy-washy approach with my clients doesn't work and they like a firm, yet encouraging attitude.

All clients complete a medical questionnaire so that I can identify if the programme is suitable for them.

A full case history is taken where I gather information

about the client's eating habits, asking them questions such as: why they eat; get them to describe a typical day with food; why they want to lose weight; how being overweight makes them feel; what do they see when they look in the mirror and how they will celebrate once weight loss has been achieved.

I will go over the Asian Exclusive 28-day meal plan step by step, outlining how they can eat Indian food in a healthy way and avoid dishes that are high in fat, such as clarified butter, Indian sweets and fried food.

I will emphasise that they should adopt a lifestyle where they eat well 80 percent of the time and 20 percent of the time they are allowed a little of what they fancy. If the client opts in for hypnosis they are put under a tailor-made trance. They are finally given three motivational tools as part of their homework to use immediately and their progress is monitored daily until the next session.

Session 2
The second session involves monitoring the client's progress and how they have got on with food.

The client is put under hypnosis to reprogramme their mind to make healthier choices with food and is given three motivational tools, such as sticking warning signs up where there is temptation with food.

One example might be: "do not reward yourself with food, you are not a dog." They will also receive a personalised hypnosis MP3 to listen to in their own time.

Session 3
In the third session I will explain if I have not seen weight loss at this point they will be taken off my programme.

So far no one has been removed as they don't want to fail. I will usually do the Swish technique in this session, but I will tailor the session according to a client's needs. I will set them another motivational tool, for example I might ask them to judge the habits of a fat person, (I will make it clear to judge the habits, not the actual person).

Session 4
Session four involves a fat aversion where they visualise how fat has been sitting on their body like lard and under hypnosis they will be releasing it from their body.

Session 5 and 6
By the time we get to session five and six the client is used to a new healthy way of eating so the last two sessions mainly revolve around adopting these changes for good.

I will use authoritarian hypnosis where the client's mind is reframed to implement the changes that have been made long term. My clients like a positive and can-do attitude which takes them to their weight loss goal much faster. I measure my success by their success and I now have so many positive stories from my clients.

Reference
The Arthritis Foundation http://ow.ly/UvjyL

Want to know more?

You can find out more about Manjit at www.yourweightlosswhippet.co.uk She is currently writing a book, Slim and Spicy, *to help the Asian community eat more healthily. This will be out early next year. You can get a recipe for a healthy curry, read a script Manjit used to help a client who had struggled with her weight for more than 30 years and read her case studies at www.yourhypnotherapyniche.com*

Index

Added value 15
Addiction definition of 57
Addictive cycle 60
Anxiety assessment 76
Anxiety, prevalence of 13
Anxiety disorders, statistics 130
Avoidance 101
Aviophobia 99
Awareness 79

Bandler R 69
Brand 6
Behaviour change 64
Blackboard technique 67
Brain and addiction 60
Brain and noise 116
Breathing technique 135
Brooding 81
Book, writing 89

Clickbank 25
Chrevreul's pendulum 77
Coaching and hypnotherapy 88
Coaching, expertise 91
Competance learning cycle 78
Competition 29

Index

Consultation, complimentary 14, 136
Corporate world, working with 74
Coue's law 76

Donmar Alice 44
Diets, failure of 162,181
Diet, learning not to 182
Digital business model 14
Distress tolerance 80

EDMR 103
Eating guidelines 172
Ellis Albert 149
Email list   10
Excuses 155, 169
Exercise, importance of 167
Executives, pressure 72

Facebook   9
Fast phobia technique 104
Fat 149
Fertility related technique 54
Fertility, client expectations 46
Focus techniques 94
Habit, origin of 66
Harvard medical school 44

Index

Healthy diet 165
Hearing, mechanics of 115

Gestalt 106
Goals 95
Goleman Daniel 79
Grinder J 69
GROW model 78

Ideal client 6
Indian food 179
Imagination 141
Infertility causes of 40
Infertility training in 49
IVF long protocol 49

Letter writing 173
Levita, Profesor 44

Markets Niche 32
Markets, choosing a 21
Markets evergreen 22
Mindset, growth, fixed 168
Myers Briggs 78

Index

Niche 5
Niche products 19

Panic attacks 132
Perfectionism 84
Portion sizes 164
Product ideas 25
PR   12
Pricing 28

Referring on 92
Reframing 102
Refunds 156

Scripts, delivery of 158
Self-esteem 83
Six step reframe 107
Solution-focused questioning 51, 91
SPADE 125
Specialist coaching 91
Stress, signs of 73
Stress, cost to companies 73
Stress, and fat 152
Supervision 88
SWISH 106

Target audience 20

Index

Tasking 139
Tinnitus, two categories 112
Tinnitus, causes of 117
Tinnitus, lifestyle 124
Transactional analysis 102
Twitter 11

USP 32

Visualisation techniques 68

Webinars 13
Website rules 7
Weightloss men 145
Weightloss excuses 151
Writing for business niche 97

Find your niche

At the Hypnotherapy Experts website

And access more useful material visit

www.yourhypnotherapyniche.com

If you have bought this book then you can get access to extra resources. Just go to the contact us page on the website and email us quoting the words "niche 2016".

the hypnotherapy experts

Printed in Great Britain
by Amazon

The Hypnotherapy Experts

Edited by Ann Jaloba HPD

the hypnotherapy experts